Integrated Family Intervention for Child Conduct Problems

A Behaviour-Attachment-Systems Intervention **for Parents**

Mark Dadds

David Hawes

University of New South Wales

AUSTRALIAN ACADEMIC PRESS
Brisbane

First published in 2006 by
Australian Academic Press Pty Ltd
32 Jeays Street
Bowen Hills QLD 4006
Australia
www.australianacademicpress.com.au

National Library of Australia
Cataloguing-in-Publication Data:

Dadds, Mark R.
Integrated family intervention for child conduct problems:
A behaviour-attachment-systems intervention for parents.

ISBN: 1 875378 58 8

1. Child mental health. 2. Behaviour therapy. 3. Family
psychotherapy. I. Hawes, David. II. Title.

362.2083

About the Authors

Mark Dadds is currently Professor of Psychology at the University of New South Wales, Australia, and Senior Research Fellow of the National Health and Medical Research Council of Australia. He was previously Co-Director of the Griffith Adolescent Forensic Assessment and Treatment Centre, and Director of Research in the School of Applied Psychology, Griffith University, Australia. He directs several national intervention programs for children, youth, and their families, at risk for mental health problems. These programs have been implemented in each state in Australia and in Canada, the United States, Belgium, and Holland. He has been National President of the Australian Association for Cognitive and Behavioural Therapy, Director of Research for the Abused Child Trust of Queensland, and a recipient of several awards, including an Early Career Award from the Division of Scientific Affairs of the Australian Psychological Society and a Violence Prevention Award from the Federal Government via the Institute of Criminology. He has authored four books and over 100 papers on child and family psychology.

David Hawes is a clinical psychologist and early career researcher. He is currently a postdoctoral fellow at the School of Psychology, University of New South Wales, Australia, where he also lectures in developmental psychology. He has published research into early intervention for conduct problems in children at risk for chronic and severe antisocial behaviour, and the clinical assessment of childhood psychopathology and parenting practices. This research has been presented at international conferences in the United States, Europe, and Australia. His clinical experience in child and family intervention encompasses community settings, controlled trials, and private practice.

Acknowledgments

We would like to offer acknowledgment and thanks to those who have contributed to this work. First, thanks to all the families who we have worked with over the years — you taught us so much. Thanks to Matt Sanders, who was an inspirational mentor to Mark Dadds, and to all those involved in behavioural family interventions in Australia and those who developed many of the ideas now common parlance in this area. Thanks also to the National Health and Medical Research Council of Australia, which has supported so much of our research.

Contents

SECTION 1:
Background to the Treatment

Introduction

Childhood conduct problems represent a major source of family distress and account for a large proportion of referrals to child and family mental health services. Conduct problems also feature in a range of childhood disorders, and in themselves represent a risk factor for various social and health problems at later stages of development. It is undoubtedly due to the high incidence and far-reaching impact of these problems that their prevention and treatment have been the subjects of intense interest for professionals involved in the care of children. This manual presents a comprehensive and efficacious family-based treatment for conduct problems, incorporating current empirical knowledge of child and family functioning and extensive clinical experience.

ABOUT THE MANUAL

The intervention covered in this manual is mainly targeted at young children two to eight years old with conduct problems such as:

- aggression
- non-compliance
- rule-breaking
- tantrums
- fighting with siblings.

This age range was determined because the intervention uses the strategy 'time-out', a technique that is appropriate only for younger children. However, with a suitable adaptation of this strategy – for example, substituting it with a more age-appropriate contingency – this intervention would also be suitable for older children. Additionally, the principles addressed in this intervention in relation to consultation with parents can be used to guide most interventions for children, as it has been shown that a family focus successfully enhances outcomes associated with treatment for anxious children (Barrett, Dadds, & Rapee, 1996).

Details of any direct assessment or intervention for children individually are not included in this manual. Ordinarily we would cover this in the second session and it would involve direct observation (and interview if the child is old enough) of the child during play and task interactions with the parent, as well as a basic assessment of cognitive and emotional functioning. In this manual we restrict ourselves to the parental aspects of the intervention. The evidence is clear that behavioural family interventions limited to the parents are efficacious for young children with conduct problems. With older children and those with other childhood disorders, child-focused interventions will typically be incorporated into the treatment program.

This treatment program can be used in a range of intervention contexts. We describe it as a face-to-face individual tertiary treatment for children referred for conduct problems. The techniques involved, however, are relevant to all parents who are struggling to manage child behaviour. As such, this and similar interventions can be used as an early intervention for families at risk, and as a universal preventive intervention for all parents, which is usually presented in group formats (see Sanders, Markie-Dadds, & Turner, 2003, for a discussion of a multilevel model of implementation).

WHO CAN USE THIS MANUAL?

Although we have tried to make the manual as comprehensive as possible, a range of therapeutic skills and knowledge are necessary to successfully implement this program. These include:

- clinical family consultation
- child development and psychopathology
- assessment methods used to appraise a child's problems
- social learning theory (especially Patterson's coercive process model; Patterson, 1982)
- attachment, family systems, and cognitive/attributional theories.

Essential also is the extensive repertoire an experienced therapist brings to therapy, such as empathy skills, a good sense of humour for coping with the full gamut of family dynamics, and a general respect for other people's views.

As such, this program may be used effectively by professionals across a range of disciplines involved with the care of children and families including:

- psychologists
- social workers
- family counsellors
- paediatricians
- psychiatrists.

BEHAVIOURAL FAMILY INTERVENTIONS

Behavioural family intervention (BFI) is recognised as one of the most widely used and empirically supported therapeutic interventions for children and families (Serketich & Dumas, 1996). It involves modifying the parenting behaviours that are hypothesised to maintain aggressive, antisocial child behaviour through coercive parent–child interchanges (Patterson, 1982). The process of this therapy involves the functional analysis of parent and child behaviours occurring in these coercive cycles, and the use of practical techniques (for example, rehearsals, modelling) to empower parents to effectively implement techniques such as praise and time-out that may have been used ineffectively in the past. While based on operant conditioning principles, it is simplistic to describe this therapy as merely a matter of modifying behavioural contingencies. The aim of this intervention is not only to improve child behaviour, but also to give parents insight into the effect that their own behaviour has on their child's behaviour, and to emphasise the importance of warmth and boundaries in the parent–child relationship.

More broadly, BFI is a collection of therapeutic processes and techniques that aim to produce positive change in a child's behaviour and adjustment through changes in those aspects of the family environment that are causally implicated in the maintenance of the child's problem behaviour. This may include attempting to change parents' behaviour, including their marital relationship, and other aspects of family functioning, such as the behaviour of siblings, grandparents, and babysitters; parents' household organisation; the division of labour among caregivers; elimination of safety hazards from a child's play environment; and the provision of age-appropriate toys and activities in the home (Sanders & Dadds, 1993). It involves systematic application of social learning principles and behavioural techniques, with an emphasis on reciprocity of change among different family members.

Over the last few decades there have been enormous and important developments in our understanding of family processes and child adjustment. Contemporary models of developmental psychopathy are more inclusive than the operant conditioning principles that drove the early models of BFI. Aspects of attachment, family structures, cognitive/attributional processes, and child temperament now feature as important considerations in both developmental models and treatment practice.

This manual describes a BFI for behavioural problems in young children. While built on tried and true behavioural principles, the intervention fine-tunes their application with attention to contemporary thinking about attachment, family structure, parental cognitions, and processes of change.

THE EFFECTIVENESS OF BEHAVIOURAL FAMILY INTERVENTIONS

The effectiveness of psychological treatments has been subject to greater scrutiny in recent years than ever before. Treatments for conduct problems are among those recently evaluated by task force inquiries for the purpose of policy-making and the development of professional guidelines (for example, Brestan & Eyberg, 1998; Farmer, Compton, Burns, & Robertson, 2002), and have been the focus of recent meta-analytic investigation (for example, Serketich & Dumas, 1996). Decades of efficacy studies have produced a rich body of evidence of the magnitude, generalisability, and duration of treatment effects for parent training, and the benefits of adjunctive and modified treatment formats.

Brestan and Eyberg (1998) conducted an influential review of empirically supported treatments for children and adolescents with conduct problems, applying criteria proposed by the Division 12 Task Force on Promotion and Dissemination of Psychological Procedures (1995). Eighty-two efficacy studies published between 1966 and 1995 were evaluated against the stringent criteria for well-established treatments (for example, manualised protocol, comparison group, random assignments, reliable measures, independent replication). Only two treatment protocols demonstrated the requisite level of empirical support to be considered well-established, both of which were parent-training interventions. Based in part on the Brestan and Eyberg (1998) review, Farmer et al. (2002) identified subsequent evidence in support of these conclusions.

The two well-established treatments identified by Brestan and Eyberg (1998) were programs based on Patterson and Gullion's (1968) manual *Living With Children* and videotape of modelling of parent training (for example, Webster-Stratton, 1994). These two 'treatments' therefore represent two categories of parent training, the first of which has been disseminated over time in many variants. The findings of this review offer a reminder that the parent-training programs in use today are based on treatment components that have remained largely unchanged since the late 1960s. Brestan and Eyberg (1998) noted, however, that the quality of evidence in support of parent-training interventions has increased over time. While this trend can be attributed in part to methodological advances in parent-training research, it also likely reflects ongoing refinement in parent-training delivery and practitioner training. With age comes experience, and in the case of parent training, contemporary treatment manuals such as this one reflect the learning that comes with years of practice.

In a meta-analysis of 26 well-controlled BFI outcome studies, Serketich and Dumas (1996) pointed out that the studies were characterised by large effects sizes. The authors calculated that in those studies, the average child treated with BFI was better-adjusted following treatment than approximately 80% of children in other treatment or control conditions. The treatment gains attributed to BFI in such well-controlled outcome studies have been demonstrated across a range of outcome criteria. These include change in diagnostic status as measured by the criteria set out in the fourth edition of the *Diagnostic and Statistical Manual of Mental Disorders* (DSM-IV; American Psychiatric Association, 1994), which is assessed through clinical interview (for example, Nixon, Sweeney, Erickson, & Touyz, 2004); a drop from the clinical to normal range on self-report instruments of externalising behaviour (for example, Webster-Stratton & Hammond, 1997); and decreases in oppositional behaviour and ineffective parenting assessed through methods of direct observation (for example, Nixon et al., 2004).

In well-controlled studies of recent years, treatment gains have been shown to be maintained at one-year follow-up in samples of four- to eight-year-olds (Webster-Stratton & Hammond, 1997) and two- to three-year-olds (Gross et al., 2003), while support for the maintenance of treatment effects at two-year follow-up in preschool-aged children has been reported by Nixon et al. (2004). While the generalisability of BFI treatment effects has been investigated less rigorously than the durability of these effects, research has demonstrated the generalisation of behavioural gains to school settings (McNeil, Eyberg, Eisenstadt, Newcomb, & Funderburk, 1991), community settings (Sanders & Glynn, 1981), and siblings of the target child (Webster-Stratton, Kolpacoff, & Hollinsworth, 1989).

As evidence of the effectiveness of parent training has grown over time, so too has knowledge of the factors associated with treatment success and failure. The literature examining predictors of poor treatment success has focused on parent and social adversity factors that are known to interfere with parenting. In the body of research, limited treatment effectiveness has been associated with a range of factors; for example, maternal depression, poor social support, marital problems, single-parent status, socioeconomic disadvantage, and negative life stresses (see Beauchaine, Webster-Stratton, & Reid, 2005). As evidence of such factors being predictors of limited treatment effectiveness has grown, behavioural interventions have been adapted to address the respective treatment barriers by the inclusion of adjunctive treatment components (for example, Miller & Prinz, 1990), the use of innovative formats for delivery (for example, Sanders, Markie-Dadds, Tully, & Bor, 2000), and the use of broader ecological interventions (for example, Henggeler, Melton, & Smith, 1992).

More recently, researchers have begun to consider the association between child characteristics and treatment outcome. The child characteristic that has been found to be the most strongly associated with treatment outcome is age, with treatment gains found to be greater in younger children (Dishion & Patterson, 1992; Ruma, Burke, & Thompson, 1996). There is also some evidence that children with more-severe and pervasive conduct problems achieve fewer behavioural improvements and less generalisation of these changes (Ruma et al., 1996; Webster-Stratton, 1996). Interestingly, studies of comorbidity have found that children with comorbid anxiety or depression benefit more from behavioural intervention for conduct problems than children without features of these disorders (Beauchaine et al., 2005). This paradoxical finding is consistent, however, with emerging evidence regarding the role of child temperament in the development of antisocial behaviour (see Frick & Morris, 2004).

In summary, BFI is an effective, relatively brief treatment for families of children with behavioural problems. Despite its effectiveness and widespread dissemination, it is clearly documented in the literature that a subset of families, usually those with multiple dysfunctions and particularly difficult children, do not benefit from it. Such families may drop out of treatment, show no change through treatment, or relapse into problems following some initial change. These problems have led to some creative adaptations of the basic model in attempts to maximise the reach and impact of the treatments; however, most treatments still rely on the same principles that drove the initial treatments in the 1960s. In the next section, we review theoretical and practical developments that critically inform how BFI can be fine-tuned to maximise its uptake, implementation, and effectiveness with difficult, multiply distressed families.

PARENT–CHILD INTERPERSONAL DYNAMICS

SOCIAL LEARNING FACTORS

There is broad consensus that the interpersonal dynamics occurring in parent–child dyads are critical to behavioural outcomes in children, both directly and in mediating the effects of other risk factors such as poverty (for example, Shaw, Bell, & Gilliom, 2000). The social learning processes used to explain these dynamics form the basis for parent-training interventions, and have guided much of the research evaluating these treatments. The advent of Patterson's (1982) coercion model was associated with major conceptual and methodological advances in the application of social learning theory to explanations of antisocial development.

In an effort to collect objective behavioural data concerning family processes, Patterson, Reid, and colleagues developed coding systems for recording the moment-to-moment interactions between parents and children during innovative, naturalistic, observational studies (see Reid, Patterson, & Snyder, 2002). These studies revealed that compared to families of children who do not have conduct problems, families of children who have conduct problems were more likely to initiate and reciprocate aggressive behaviour, and to persist in aversive behaviour once they had initiated it. Such families were described as highly coercive social systems, in which all family members contributed to bilateral and systemic coercion in relation to the target child (Snyder & Stoolmiller, 2002).

Patterson (1982) proposed that two main processes were operating in such families, and that these could be explained using operant conditioning principles. The first of these processes is the parental modelling of antisocial or aggressive behaviour. The second process involves 'reinforcement traps', which can occur in a variety of ways. A common chain of actions would involve a parent making an intrusive request of a child, the child protesting with aversive behaviour, and the parent then capitulating. In such an example, the child's aversive behaviour is positively reinforced by the parent's capitulation, which in turn is negatively reinforced by the termination of the child's aversive behaviour. In an alternative reinforcement trap, the more a child engages in undesirable behaviours, the less likely it is that the child will be reinforced for positive behaviours. Parents who develop aversive associations with child interaction due to experiences related to problem behaviours will avoid involvement with the child and therefore be less attentive to positive child behaviours. Evidence in support of these processes has been reported in decades of observational studies (see review by Snyder & Stoolmiller, 2002), and a range of efficacious behavioural interventions have flowed directly from this model (see McMahon & Forehand, 2003; Sanders & Dadds, 1993; Webster-Stratton & Hancock, 1998). The application of operant principles to parent–child interactive therapies must be considered one of the most potent innovations of the mental health sciences.

> In this program, training parents in the effective use of social learning contingencies for managing problem behaviour in children remains the cornerstone of the treatment. However, as noted below, our approach is greatly tempered by placing the use of these contingencies in attachment, structural, and cognitive attributional frameworks.

ATTACHMENT

While the construct of attachment represents a relatively minor focus within the antisocial development literature, the contributions of attachment theory have received growing attention in recent years, and the integration of such theory with broader, social learning–based models appears to be an emerging trend (for example, Dadds, 2002; Lyons-Ruth, 1996; Shaw et al., 2000). The essence of classical attachment theory (Ainsworth, Blehard, Waters, & Wall, 1978; Bowlby, 1969) is that all humans have an innate drive to attach to a caregiving figure. Where the caregiver reciprocates with predictable nurturance, the child establishes a secure, trusting attachment that allows them to confidently explore the environment, safe in the knowledge that the caregiver is available should nurturance be needed. Insecure attachment occurs when the caregiver is unavailable or unpredictable in their nurturance. Avoidant patterns occur when the child refrains from contact with the caregiver, anxious/ambivalent patterns occur when the child escalates clinging behaviour in order to avoid the anxiety of caregiver non-availability, and disorganised patterns show a mix of insecure styles. Children with behavioural problems are less likely to show secure attachments than their healthy peers; however, research into these characteristics is scarce (see Lyons-Ruth, 1996, for a review). Studies of middle-class samples have found associations between externalising behaviour and avoidant attachment patterns (for example, Erickson, Sroufe, & Egeland, 1985); however, it appears that disorganised attachment patterns are more strongly related to aggressive behaviour in populations characterised by broader risk factors. Infants with disorganised attachment patterns may exhibit unpredictable alternations of approach and avoidance, and a range of helpless, depressed, or aggressive behaviours (Greenberg, Speltz, & DeKlyen, 1993; Lyons-Ruth, Alpern, & Repacholi, 1993; Lyons-Ruth, Repacholi, McLeod, & Silva, 1991).

Attachment studies of fathers have been rare (Lamb, 1997); however, such research has made important contributions to knowledge of the role that fathers play in the development of conduct problems. Consistent with findings for infant–mother attachment, insecure attachments with fathers have been associated with peer problems at age five (Youngblade & Belsky, 1992), as well as increased likelihood of referral for early onset conduct problems (DeKlyen, Speltz, & Greenberg, 1998). Evidence of processes more specific to infant–father attachments has been provided by the study of adult attachment histories, as measured using the Adult Attachment Interview (Bakermans-Kranenburg & van IJzendoorn, 1993). In a non-clinical sample of three-and-a-half-year-olds, Cowan, Cohn, Cowan, and Pearson (1996) found that fathers' attachment history was a better predictor of teacher-rated externalising behaviour than mothers' attachment history. Alternatively, mothers' attachment history was a better predictor of internalising symptoms.

While the integration of attachment theory into social learning models of antisocial behaviour represents a relatively new idea, the similarities between attachment theory and social learning models of antisocial behaviour can be traced back to classic experiments in psychology. Dadds (2002) noted that a largely forgotten series of animal experiments conducted by Harlow and Harlow in 1962 elucidate the role that attachment may play in relation to processes such as those in Patterson's coercion model. In these experiments, comfort and food (as well as aversive stimuli) were delivered to an infant monkey through a mechanical mother monkey. The authors described approach–avoidance conflicts in these dyads, with the delivery of aversive stimuli from the mother resulting in increased clinging behaviour rather than avoidance from the infant, a pattern closely related to anxious/ambivalent attachment.

In human families, it could be assumed that such clinging behaviour from the infant would elicit comforting behaviours in the mother, as well as reactions of displeasure when the clinging behaviour is excessive. Reactions of displeasure and rejecting behaviours would, in turn, increase the likelihood of further aversive clinging behaviour from the infant. Such a vicious circle is very similar to that described by Patterson's coercion theory. Thus, in extreme cases, the parent and child could become trapped in a cycle of proximity-seeking and rejection, with the child developing an increasingly aversive set of (mis)behaviours to attract the attention of the caregiver. Dadds (2002) describes this cycle as escalating until aversive discipline interchanges between the parent and child become increasingly frequent and attachment-'rich'. That is, they contain all sorts of interchanges relevant to basic attachment drives in the child and, naturally, the child will continue to escalate. In this model, the child is misbehaving not for attention per se, but for all the attachment-rich dynamics the discipline interchanges bring.

On the contrary, positive interchanges between the parent and child become increasingly scarce and attachment-neutral. That is, they rarely involve predictable love and nurturance. We see many families in our clinic who have been trained in the traditional BFI way to use rewarding strategies for positive child behaviour, and a time-out procedure for misbehaviour for whom the treatment has not worked due to the above problems. The rewarding strategies (for example, descriptive praise) are still attachment-neutral and the discipline procedure is still attachment-rich.

Time-out is a good example of how incorporating attachment principles into child management strategies can improve their effectiveness. If time-out is used in a rejecting and unpredictable way, it presents an attachment threat to the child that will lead to further problems. The threat to the child can be understood in terms of attachment theory and also models of ostracism. Williams and Zadro (2001) have shown that ostracism has a serious and immediate biological and psychological impact that can result in a range of aggressive and withdrawn/depressed behaviours. On the other hand, time-out is not a threat to attachments, and one is not ostracised by time-out. That is, it is simply a mild punishment that predictably follows the misbehaviour that led to its use.

In this program, the ideas of attachment-rich and attachment-neutral parenting are applied to strategies to manage positive child behaviour and misbehaviour, respectively. That is, we aim to reverse the typical profile of a family who has a child with a conduct problem by making parent responses to positive child behaviour attachment-rich and responses to problem behaviour attachment-neutral.

FAMILY STRUCTURE

There is little evidence that family structures are a direct causal variable in child problems; however, there is clear evidence that family structures operate as a broad risk factor for both the development of problem behaviours and poor responses to traditional behavioural parent interventions (see Dadds, 1995). Thus, families in which the parents are in conflict or separated can fare badly in both regards. More subtly, family hierarchies that are badly organised can exacerbate child problems and make working with such families very difficult. Green, Loeber, and Lahey (1992) showed that hierarchical structures tend to become disorganised in families of children who behave problematically; typically, boundaries between parent, child, and extended family systems become unclear; the parents' relationship becomes conflicted; and extended family may get caught in the battles during the many failed attempts to manage the child who is behaving problematically.

While the ideas of Salvatore Minuchin and the other structural family theorists have attracted little attention in empirical studies, their ideas can be of considerable use in determining how to engage and manage problematic family structures. According to Minuchin (1974), a healthy family is characterised by overlapping but independent parenting, child, and extended family systems. Most importantly, the parents act as an executive system, have a positive relationship independent of the parenting roles, and can function effectively to solve family problems. In contrast, many parents of children who have conduct problems are beset with their own relationship problems, cannot deal with problems as a team, and find themselves split and estranged in their attempts to manage the children. Several studies have shown that targeting this teamwork aspect of parental relationships can enhance the outcomes associated with parent training for child conduct problems (Dadds, Sanders, Behrens, & James, 1987; Dadds, Schwartz, & Sanders, 1987).

In the treatment model we use, close attention is paid to facilitating positive family structures, especially a loving and effective parental subsystem, both in terms of the content of training and the way family treatment sessions are structured.

COGNITIVE ATTRIBUTIONAL PROCESSES

A wealth of research has shown that parents of children with conduct problems develop problematic attributions about the meaning of the child's behaviour (for example, Dadds, Mullins, McAllister, & Atkinson, 2003). Common examples include the parent feeling that the child's behaviour is intentional and under the child's control, is designed to deliberately upset the parent, is a sign of serious mental problems, is inherited from other (disliked) family members (for example, an abusive ex-spouse), or is in some way a punishment that the parent deserves. Further, parents may be horrified by the thoughts and impulses of rejection and hatred that they sometimes have about the child. Finally, parents may have beliefs about models of discipline that are incompatible with the operant techniques typically taught in parent-training programs. All of these cognitions can make it very difficult to calmly parent a child and are a risk factor for failure to implement traditional parent-training programs (for example, Wahler & Dumas, 1989).

Parents' cognitions about the meaning of their child's behaviour, their own feelings about the child, and their beliefs about discipline are explicitly targeted for assessment and intervention in this model of intervention.

THE PROCESS OF CONSULTATION

It does not matter how effective a therapy is if parents do not implement it. As such, successfully managing the process of consultation is a necessary condition for effective change. Little is available in the empirical parent-training literature to guide the consultation process; however, that information which exists is informative. Patterson and Chamberlain (1994) showed that parent engagement and cooperation is best enhanced through use of a stage model in which didactic input is suspended until client trust is built by giving parents adequate time to express their concerns in supportive, client-centred sessions. Sanders and Dadds (1993) similarly emphasise a stage model in which the therapist and parents form a team, jointly lead the assessment process, and then develop a shared perception of the problem and potential solutions prior to any treatment taking place. In this treatment program, the therapy process emphasises teamwork, parent empowerment, and support right from the first contact with the family through to termination. First, careful attention is paid to the structuring of the first session in terms of who attends; how the interview is structured; and how 'hot' topics such as violence, marital relationship, drugs, the parents' feelings for the child, and so on are raised and dealt with. Second, throughout the treatment we emphasise the establishment of a therapeutic team in which the parents and the therapist are all experts who have different yet complementary skills. This has important implications for how the therapist responds to any signs of client resistance, a common problem in parent-training programs. Rather than thinking of resistance as a problem, we reformulate it as an important communication from the parent. Thus, rather than trying to argue down parental doubts about treatment, failure to complete tasks, and other challenges, in this program the therapist actively encourages the client to express their concerns and thanks the client for doing so, leading the team to think about how to adapt the program to address the client's concerns.

> The process of consultation is critical to the success of therapy. The current model emphasises the formation of an equal partnership with parents, the avoidance of defensive and didactic responses in the face of parental resistance, and the adoption of a flexible stage model of consultation that moves smoothly between client-centred and didactic therapist behaviours.

THE TREATMENT MODEL

Our literature review and clinical experience with hundreds of children with conduct problems and their families has led us to put forward a treatment model that expands upon the traditional behavioural parent-training model by integrating the following theoretical tools into the conceptualisation of both the child's problems and the strategies for intervention:

SOCIAL LEARNING THEORY

Social learning theory focuses on the specific contingencies that characterise parent–child interactions and is the hallmark of all empirically supported interventions for children with conduct problems.

ATTACHMENT THEORY

In this treatment program, we use the constructs of attachment-rich and attachment-neutral parent–child interactions. On the one hand, in families of children with conduct problems, positive interactions become increasingly scarce and are typically attachment-neutral; that is, they offer little in the way of love and acceptance towards the child. However, this does not mean that the parents are to blame for this. They, like the child, are often trapped in a coercive system in which the daily toll of dealing with misbehaviour leaves them with little positive emotions and behaviour left to give. Even parents who have been trained in positive parenting fall short of exhibiting lots of attachment-rich behaviour as they restrict their positive interactions to the use of (attachment-neutral) praise and other artificial rewards. In this treatment program, we focus on ensuring that the interactions applied to non-problematic child behaviour are rich in love, acceptance, and shared time. That is, we expand upon traditional training of parents in skills for reinforcing appropriate child behaviour by emphasising that such positive interactions are and should be driven by positive, secure, attachment-rich behaviour. Thus, the use of tokens and other artificial rewards are replaced by a focus on love, intimacy, and acceptance.

On the other hand, in families of children who are behaving problematically, discipline scenarios are typically attachment-rich. That is, the child's misbehaviour can drive the parent to invest large amounts of time in dealing with the child, which can often escalate to the parents exhibiting rejection behaviour, isolating themselves from each other, threatening separation, and so on. A child will naturally choose attachment-rich over attachment-neutral parent behaviour and, in the above circumstances, the child who is misbehaving will continue to misbehave in order to provoke attachment-rich parent behaviour. Thus, in this treatment program, we use attachment-neutral parenting to characterise interactions with the child when they are behaving badly. That is, the parent learns to manage misbehaviour without provoking attachment issues.

STRUCTURAL FAMILY ISSUES

Families struggling with a child who has conduct problems often find that they become increasingly fragmented into problematic alliances. Parents find that their relationship suffers and that their children become aggressive with each other, and extended family members often find themselves taking sides. We draw upon Salvatore Minuchin's (1974) idea that a healthy family is roughly structured around a core parenting team (executive role), a child system, and an extended family system. Thus, parents have a relationship that is not split by members of the other systems and therefore they can function effectively to support and love each other as well as solve problems that beset the broader system. In the intervention we use, attention is paid to ensuring that the structure of sessions as well as the content of the intervention enhances the parenting system.

COGNITIVE ATTRIBUTIONAL ISSUES

A vast literature base shows that parents often develop negative attributions about the meaning of their child's problematic behaviour. Thus, they may harbour all sorts of beliefs about their child's character: the problematic behaviour is deliberate, a sign of mental illness, evil, inherited from other (disliked) family members, and so on. Parents of children who behave problematically can also feel terrible about the thoughts they harbour about the child. They expect that they will love their children unconditionally; however, at times they find themselves despairing about the child, perhaps even experiencing hatred and resentment. Unless parents are helped to make these thoughts explicit, accept them, and move forward, it will be very difficult for them to implement day-to-day management strategies that require calm processing of the child's behaviour. This intervention focuses on these problematic thoughts from the first session onwards.

Optimal outcomes in behavioural family interventions are contingent upon a number of factors. For effective practice of behavioural parent training it is necessary to have both an understanding of process issues and the skills required to manage these issues.

ASSESSMENT

The assessment stage is integral to any intervention involving the application of behavioural principles. In this program, assessment is conducted with attention to a number of process issues typically encountered in family interventions. The appropriate negotiation of these issues will not only facilitate the accurate and efficient collection of assessment information, but also lay the foundations for the therapeutic work that follows.

Over the years, we have observed hundreds of videotaped sessions of trainee therapists. By noting the commonalities of cases that drop out of treatment or fail to implement procedures, we have identified several typical therapeutic 'hot spots' in which the consultation process is likely to fail, either obviously or in subtle ways that not even the therapist really notices. These include the following:

FAILURE TO ESTABLISH WHO SHOULD ATTEND THE SESSION AND WHY

The consultation process can fail if in the first session the therapist does not establish a good working relationship with the parents because of insufficient thought about who should attend the session and why. A common reason for not establishing a good working relationship is having parents and children attend the whole of the first session together so that the therapist is unable to hold a truly parent-centred session that involves focusing on the parents' relationship, any controversial family issues, how the parents truly feel about the child, and so on. Many therapists trained in family-systems approaches believe that the first session should involve all family members so that the system as a whole can be observed. This does not allow the parents to vent their feelings without the possibility of harming the child, and is not consistent with our model of first setting up the parents as an executive team. At worst, we have seen initial sessions in which the child's (or children's) problem behaviour has escalated and the session has been a disaster. As a general principle, we recommend starting the consultation process with the parents or parent alone in order to allow them the space to vent on all relevant issues and set up plans for treatment as an adult team. Observations of the broader system and interaction patterns can follow in subsequent sessions once this necessary working relationship is established.

FAILURE TO ESTABLISH A GOOD WORKING RELATIONSHIP WITH BOTH *PARENTS*

The consultation process can fail if in the first session the therapist does not establish a trusting relationship with *both* parents (if there are two). An example of a scenario that can easily lead to this is as follows. A mother describes her problems with her six-year-old son, and when the father is asked for his views he attacks the mother's handling of the boy, arguing that the boy has no problems but that the mother is to blame for her nitpicking parenting style. When confronted by such a scenario, most new therapists instinctively move to protect the mother, subtly advocating for her in an attempt to bring some reason and compassion to the father. While this response is understandable, it often does not help and leads to the father feeling that the therapist (usually a female as well) is siding with the mother. Consequently, the father drops out of therapy or pulls the family out of therapy, or he continues with the therapy but undermines the process. In this treatment program, we guide the therapist to pay careful attention to making sure that all members of the family feel heard and respected no matter how outrageous their views are, and to integrate the views of all family members into the larger conceptualisation. It is surprising how extreme views are retracted and empathy increased all round once a person has felt that they have been heard.

FAILURE TO SENSITIVELY RAISE DIFFICULT ISSUES

The consultation process can fail if difficult issues such as abuse and violence, family members' feelings for each other, parental attributions about the child's behaviour and problems, use of drugs and alcohol, and the role of extended family members are either not raised or are done so in a way that results in the parents feeling as though they are being blamed for them. In a successful first session, these issues will have been raised sensitively but explicitly and then integrated into the overall conceptualisation that is jointly formulated by the therapist and family.

FAILURE TO DEVELOP A SHARED CONCEPTUALISATION AND TREATMENT PLAN

The consultation process can fail if after the assessment the therapist's conceptualisation and resulting treatment plan is not truly a joint exercise in which the parents and therapist develop a shared perception of what the problems are and what the plan is to tackle them. Some ideas we use to facilitate this process are:

- 'not owning the data' – the therapist genuinely allows the family full access to assessment information, even going as far as putting assessment results (score sheets and so on) in the hands of parents and inviting them to interpret them and comment on them
- including the parents' perceptions as the first and most important piece of data
- using language that is common to parents and the therapist, thereby reinforcing agreement and a joint vision
- listening to and even thanking parents for expressing concerns and doubts, and setting up objective, agreeable ways of choosing between alternative explanations.

By paying careful attention to these issues, the session in which assessment information is shared and a shared perception and treatment plan is developed marks a watershed point in the consultation process. We have observed many inexperienced therapists march on valiantly into treatment despite the fact that it was clear the parents were not at all convinced about the conceptualisation or the treatment plan. This approach is a 'trust me' one, with the therapist implicitly taking the lead role as the expert. We suggest not moving forward while the parents seem doubtful, and instead empower them to make active choices about what they want to do.

FACILITATING THE INVOLVEMENT OF RELEVANT FAMILY MEMBERS IN TREATMENT

The primary aim of parent training is to shape the behaviour of those who have the most frequent contact with the referred child. In doing so, the therapist facilitates changes in the family system, the environment in which the child lives and develops. Within such a model, parents function as agents of change, making their involvement and cooperation throughout treatment critical. Accordingly, it is advantageous for both of the child's parents or caregivers to be engaged in treatment.

The likelihood of both parents participating in treatment is often diminished by parental disagreement regarding the extent to which they feel that professional help is necessary. For example, a mother may present with a child and the message that the father is not interested or is unwilling to be involved. Where an important family member initially refuses to attend, it is advisable to obtain permission from the present family members to telephone them regarding their involvement. In rare cases, some parents have refused permission, arguing that the spouse's involvement in the family is minimal and their participation in therapy would be destructive. Such a view should be addressed with gentle pressure in the form of information about the importance of both parents' roles. If the parent maintains their position, it should be accepted. In most cases, however, the parent is happy for the spouse to be contacted.

When telephoning the absent family member, the therapist can point out that they need that person's help. That is, each family member is considered an expert (the role of expert is equally assigned to all family members) who has firsthand knowledge of the family's style and the child's problems, and ideas about what sort of treatment might be implemented given the style and routine of the particular family. Few family members refuse to make at least one appointment to discuss the family's problem when this approach is used.

DEVELOPING A SHARED PERCEPTION WITH DIFFERENT FAMILY MEMBERS

It is argued here that the establishment of a facilitative relationship between the therapist and family members is a critical factor in enabling parents to explore the relationship between the child's problems and their management of the problems, and between the child's problems and contextual factors such as marital distress. Viewing family problems in an interactional or systemic way can often result in therapists inadvertently failing to form such a relationship with parents of children with a behaviour disorder. If parents begin treatment, as they often do, by complaining and blaming the child, the therapist may quickly focus on the parents' management techniques or, worse, shift focus on to other problems in the family in order to develop a focus on the family system and avoid blaming the child, rather than focus on establishing a facilitative relationship with the parents.

Many parents will perceive these lines of questioning as an implicit communication that they are to blame for the child's problems. Countless parents have dropped out of treatment because they felt the therapist blamed them for the child's problems. Ironically, most parents do tend to blame themselves, or at least wonder if they are to blame. They will communicate this in the context of a supportive relationship, but often deny it by dropping out of treatment if the confrontation is done without an initial acceptance of their perception of the problem.

An approach that commonly results in therapists making the above mistakes is that of seeing parents and children together in the first interview. Thus, if the parents openly complain about the child in their presence, the therapist may not feel able to fully explore the problem with the parents without further distressing the child and appearing to align with the parents. For this reason, the initial interview in this treatment program is conducted without children present. It should be recognised that such an approach is at variance with the approach traditionally advocated by many family therapists, who recommend having all family members present. More and more therapists are, however, recognising the benefits of splitting the family system at various times and for various reasons. During initial interviews, it can be useful to build relationships with the parents and children separately and not proceed to more-formal assessments of parent–child patterns of interaction until open and trusting relationships with all family members have been established.

FACILITATING THE DISCUSSION OF RELEVANT TOPICS

When progressing through the components of the initial interview, a consistent method should be used to facilitate the introduction and discussion of each new topic (for example, presenting problem, history of presenting problem, child health and development). This method utilises a funnelling pattern (see figure below) in which new topics are approached first with broad, open-ended, general inquiry questions. The specificity of questions should increase as the topic is addressed further by an increasing use of closed-ended questions. Such a method allows parents to present their ideas and opinions freely while also enabling an account of relevant aspects of each topic in appropriate detail. At the end of each topic key details are briefly summarised before progressing to the next.

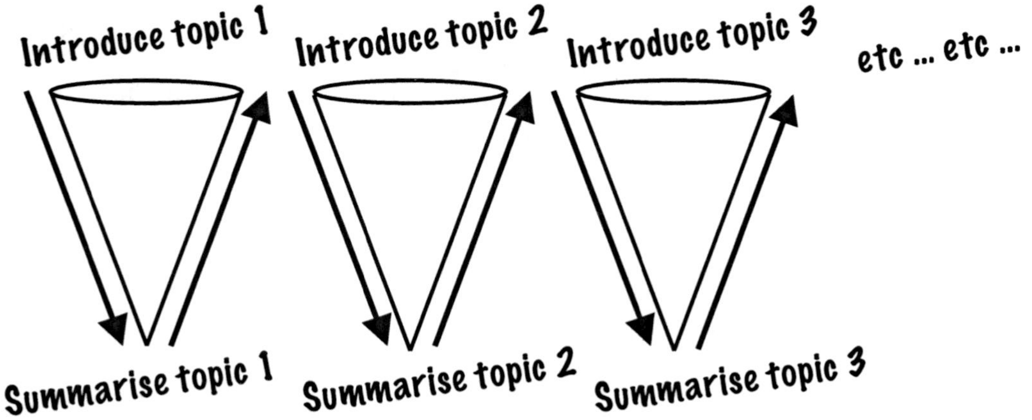

INTEGRATING THE FAMILY CONTEXT WITH THE CHILD'S PROBLEM

During the process of initial interviewing, it is important to explore and identify any issues that may be adversely impacting on the family system. Such issues may be sensitive, highly emotional, or frightening to clients. These hot topics should always be addressed in a way that maintains and maximises the client–therapist relationship, the dignity and self-esteem of the client, and the quality of the information obtained.

Problems with relating contextual aspects of family functioning (marital issues, financial stress, cultural differences) to a child's problems usually lie at two extremes. At the one extreme, problems can arise when a therapist does not raise these issues for discussion, perhaps due to fear of confronting intimate family details or due to conceptual biases about the role of these variables. At the other extreme, problems can occur when these issues are raised in such a way that causes the parents to deny their importance, existence, or the right of the therapist to focus on them.

Suggestions for effectively raising questions about family functioning are as follows:

- Inquire about other areas of family functioning only after the parents' concerns about the child have been adequately addressed.
- Make the transition from the child focus to the broader family focus as smooth as possible, preferably with a summary of the points that were discussed about the child and a brief explanation of why the therapist is also interested in the broader family.

- Err on the side of caution by asking about marital/family issues in the context of how they are affected by the child's problems rather than to what extent they have caused the child's problems.

For example, a useful way to raise the question of marital functioning and its relationship to the child's problems involves two basic steps. First, the therapist should summarise information about the child's problems to show that they have fully attended to the parents' perceptions of the child. Following this, the therapist can make a statement about how dealing with difficult child behaviour can place considerable stress on the rest of the family and in particular on the marriage, and ask the parents to discuss this as it applies to them.

When exploring such issues, the therapist should funnel questions in a similar way to the process used for progressing through the components of the broader intake interview; that is, the therapist should proceed from the general (open-ended questions) to the specific (clarification, elaboration). This process should be conducted in a way that is client-centred and that develops a shared perception of these aspects of family functioning. It can be quite easy to gradually move emphasis from child problems causing marital distress to a more reciprocal conceptualisation as the discussion continues. In fact, many parents will themselves raise the issue of the blame for the child's problems and identify certain stressors that they have created for their child at this time. With some families it may be clear that the marriage is basically sound and that the parents are jointly committed to the marriage. Alternatively, it may be indicated that the parent–child conflict is straining the parental relationship in the context of an otherwise harmonious family.

During this discussion, it is important to integrate parents' reports with other forms of assessment regarding family functioning. It is not unknown for parents to report absolutely no problem during this discussion, but to report problems such as marital distress on relevant inventories. Any discrepancies should be addressed with careful consideration of the individuals concerned. It can occur that one parent is coerced by the other into not talking about any problems except those concerning the child. Confronting parents with this information within a session, however, may increase the risk of marital friction following the session or subsequent drop-out from therapy. In such cases, it may be advisable to schedule a visit with the spouse reporting marital distress (or depression and so on) alone, perhaps in the context of assessing the child, to assess the extent of conflict, violence, and the possible implications of discussing these issues openly.

PLANNING AND INITIATING BEHAVIOURAL FAMILY INTERVENTIONS

The tasks that follow assessment consist of the scheduling, sequencing, and integrating of interventions. At this point, it is assumed that the family has established an open, trusting relationship with the therapist, and that the child has been assessed as exhibiting behaviour problems warranting a family intervention.

Before commencing treatment it is important to consider the appropriateness of intervening in systemic issues that may be contributing to problematic child behaviour as well as other difficulties. These may include psychopathologies of the parent (for example, depression, alcohol abuse), social adversity issues (for example, financial stress, poor social support), or discord within the family system (for example, marital conflict, interference from relatives). To varying degrees, such problems may represent barriers to effective treatment. Prior to progressing to the treatment, a careful decision must be made regarding the appropriateness of commencing an intervention targeting the parenting of the referred child. If it is apparent that the parents' problems are likely to significantly interfere with their participation in the treatment, it may be necessary to defer child-focused treatment and first attend to the parents' other problems. Alternatively, if such problems are considered significant but unlikely to preclude the parents' adherence to a parent-training program, the conduct problems of the referred child should remain the focus of attention. This treatment program incorporates a flexible component designed to address such problems.

In the case of marital conflict, the parents can be asked to consider whether they can co-operate sufficiently – that is, put their marital problems aside for a few weeks while they and the therapist work together as a team to help the child. It should be noted that this should be addressed in such a way that results in the parents 'owning' the decision, and not in a way in which the therapist makes directions about the role of the parents' marital problems. Clinical experience indicates that very few families will say that they cannot cooperate for a few weeks. If they report they cannot, the therapist will need to focus on the reasons for this and perhaps proceed to marital counselling prior to focusing on parenting issues. In the majority of cases, however, parents will agree to try to work as a team, thus calling a 'moratorium' on marital problems while they implement treatment for the child. It has been found that involvement in this decision can be of great benefit itself in improving family relations.

SECTION 2:
The Treatment

Session 1: Assessment With Parents

Major Component

■ **COMPREHENSIVE ASSESSMENT WITH PARENTS**

The process issues detailed in the introduction of this manual should be carefully noted for this session. These include establishing that parents are a working team, and making each parent feel as if their story has been heard, respected, and integrated into the shared perception of the problem. It is crucial that the therapist structure the conversation so that all participants have space to speak and be heard.

WELCOME AND AGENDA

Parents should be made to feel appreciated for attending the session, and punctual arrival should be reinforced with some words of gratitude. Such attention to welcoming parents should be maintained throughout treatment.

A simple agenda is proposed to parents at the commencement of each session. The agendas that appear throughout this manual are suggested based on the respective session plans, and phrased in the basic terms appropriate for this purpose. The opening statements suggested in these session plans also include explanations and descriptions considered important to establishing a shared focus for the session, and promoting client engagement and motivation. A suggested agenda for Session 1 is as follows:

> Today I'd like to form a clear and complete picture of [child's name] by asking a range of questions about the current problems he's having and about his background, such as his development. For us to decide on the best way to proceed, it's also important for me to find out about yourselves and the rest of your family. Because we'll try to cover as much ground as possible today, and because it's important that we also have time to discuss questions that you both have, we may not have time to go into any one area in too much detail.

INTERVIEW COMPONENTS

CHILD AND FAMILY DETAILS

There are various basic child and family details that the therapist should be familiar with from the outset of the initial interview. Of these, those that are known to the therapist prior to the commencement of the initial interview (for example, those that were listed on the referral form) should be clarified during the initial interview. Any outstanding details should be collected efficiently with appropriate closed-ended questions.

Child Details

- Name and age of the referred child
- The child's current school, grade, and teacher

Parent Details

- Names and ages of parents
- Occupational details (that is, type of work and whether it is full-time, part-time, or other)

Structure of the Family

- Names and ages of other relevant immediate and extended family members
- Relevant circumstances related to previous marriages (for example, step-parents, half-siblings)

Individuals (Non-Family) in the Home

- Names, ages, and circumstances related to other individuals who are not family members and are currently living with the child's family

Childcare Arrangements

- Circumstances related to childminding, including the frequency, duration, and number of individuals or services involved (including extended family)
- The frequency, duration, and history of any access visits

THE PRESENTING PROBLEM

Using an open-ended question, invite parents to describe the problems they hope to address during therapy. For example:

> What are your main concerns with Aaron?

The aim at this point is to achieve a picture of the problem in appropriate detail. This is done using selective closed-ended questions and by asking parents to describe specific examples. For example:

> What do you mean by aggressive?
>
> What happened the last time he behaved this way?

Enquire about any problems commonly associated with oppositional behaviour (for example, physical aggression) if they have not already been addressed in the course of the discussion. When broaching each type of behaviour, begin with a general enquiry question, and follow this by asking for an example (for example, the most recent incident). While it is important to clarify any ambiguities in parents' descriptions of their child's behaviour, it can be helpful to use parents' own words (for example, 'wilful', 'stubborn') when paraphrasing such descriptions. Elicit details of the problem behaviours by inviting parents to present a sequential report of what occurred during a recent incident, and check if this is typical of that type of situation.

Determine the topographical dimensions of each problem presented. Ask direct questions regarding the approximate frequency, duration, setting, and impact of the problem behaviours, in addition to the contexts in which they are observed. For example:

How often is that happening?

How long can that carry on for? Shortest time? Longest time? Average time?

What settings is he behaving like that in?

How much is this interfering with things at home/school/with peers?

Summarise identified problems before proceeding. For example:

So, your main concern is Aaron's physical and verbal aggression, and both of these things are happening on a daily basis at home. It doesn't seem to be a problem in any other setting, but it's really starting to disrupt different routines, and you're also worried that his brother is starting to copy him.

THE HISTORY OF THE REPORTED PROBLEMS

Enquiry into the history of the problem should include the approximate date of onset, and whether this onset was sudden or gradual. The chronological development of the problem is also relevant, and can be established using closed-ended questions regarding changes observed since onset. For example:

When did you first become aware of this behaviour?

Did it seem to come about suddenly, or do you think it began gradually?

How has it changed since then?

Has it become more frequent or more of a problem?

Have there been periods since it began when it hasn't been a problem?

CHILD HEALTH AND DEVELOPMENTAL HISTORY

Assess the developmental history of the referred child, addressing the relevant stages of development in appropriate detail. Ask closed questions pertaining to the issues of relevance at each stage, identifying respective problems or delays. Additionally, determine whether the child currently suffers from significant health problems or identified disabilities, or whether any such problems have occurred in the past.

Relevant developmental stages and issues in each stage include the following:

Pregnancy, Delivery, and the Neonatal Period

- Planned or unplanned
- Complications during pregnancy or delivery

Infancy

- Feeding
- Sleeping
- Crying
- Walking and talking
- Attachments

Toddlerhood

- Toilet-training
- Activity levels
- Attachments

Preschool Age

- Social behaviour
- Ability to cope with various structures and routines

Middle Childhood

- Commencement of school
- Relationships with peers and teachers
- Disruptive behaviours

GENERAL FUNCTIONING OF THE CHILD

The broader functioning of the child is explored next, including social and school-related functioning. When broaching topics in each area, begin with a general open enquiry (for example, 'What do you know about John's behaviour at school?'), and follow through with closed-ended questions as appropriate (for example, 'Does he act that way towards other adults at school, or only his music teachers?'). Once each topic has been explored, shift the discussion to the next one. For example:

> I'm getting a good picture of what his behaviour has been like. I'd like to now ask about some other common problems, which may or may not be relevant to him.

Conclude the discussion of the child's broader functioning by checking that all relevant problems have been identified. If different subclinical problems are identified in addition to significant conduct problems, explain to parents that it may be useful to address the child's conduct problems before progressing to other problem areas. Invite comments regarding this proposition.

Social Functioning

Establish whether the child's peer relationships are appropriate in terms of quality and number. If relevant, explore how peers fit into the reported pattern of conduct problems (for example, 'Is it always the same children that he is getting into trouble with?').

School Functioning

Relevant aspects of school functioning include the child's academic performance, their interpersonal behaviour and relationships with peers, and their interactions with adults. It is also relevant to determine if the child's schooling history has been disrupted by any events (for example, frequent changes of schools), and the reasons for such disruptions. It may be relevant to collect the names of previous schools and teachers and obtain parent permission to make contact for assessment purposes.

TREATMENT HISTORY

Ask the parents whether they have previously accessed treatment or therapeutic intervention for the reported problems or any previous problems. Enquire as to the form and duration of any treatment undertaken, and the outcome of the intervention. It is also important here to establish whether the child has experienced any significant psychiatric or psychological disturbances in the past, and to gather information about any associated treatment.

FAMILY RELATIONSHIPS AND PSYCHOSOCIAL DETAILS

Shift the topic of discussion to that of the broader family system. For example:

> I'd now like to ask some questions about your family so that I can see the bigger picture and get an understanding of the circumstances relevant to your child and your family.

A number of topics are to be discussed with each parent. Address these topics in a similar order with each parent, concluding the discussion with one parent before commencing with the other.

After these systemic factors have been addressed with both parents, conclude the discussion by explicitly thanking the parents for the disclosures they have made, and emphasising that such information is important to planning how to best address the problems raised.

Parent Health and Wellbeing

Assess the parent's current health and general functioning, including any past disturbances to mood or functioning. If relevant, enquire about previous treatment, identifying the form, duration, and outcome of the intervention. For example:

> Do you have any serious health problems at the moment?
>
> How's your life at the moment, more generally?
>
> How do you feel you're coping with things at the moment?

Parent Social Support

Enquire about the parent's general functioning and social support. For example:

> What kind of support do you have from friends or family?
>
> Do you have time away from the children when you spend time with adults?

The Childcare Contributions of Each Parent

Assess the extent to which each parent is involved in parenting matters. For example:

> How is the parenting workload divided between both of you?

Assess whether each parent is spending individual time with the child. For example:

> How much time would you usually spend with Aaron, just the two of you?

The Parent's Feelings and Thoughts About the Child

Rather than assuming that parents regard their child with unconditional love, enquire openly about the parent's feelings towards their child. For example:

> **How would you describe your feelings for him at the moment?**

Invite parents to share their greatest concerns about their child and their child's behaviour. For example:

> **What's your worst fear about that kind of 'devilish' side you've spoken about?**

Parent responses to such an enquiry may include anticipated problems or catastrophic thoughts, and may involve intense emotions. Fears and concerns presented by parents should be empathically acknowledged, normalised, and explored openly.

The Parent's Own Childhood

Enquire about the parent's own childhood behaviour, establishing if behaviours or traits similar to those of the referred child were apparent in the parent when they were a child themselves. For example:

> **What were you like as a little boy?**
>
> **Are there ways that you were similar to Aaron when you were a child?**

Throughout this discussion about the parent's own childhood, some attention should be given to acknowledging that most traits, even those associated with disruptive behaviour, are not necessarily negative. Such traits can often have associated strengths. For example, a boy described as bossy might also be thought of as good at organising others or standing up for himself. This can also be a good point to ask parents about the kinds of parenting or discipline methods that were used by their own parents. It can be useful for parents to understand that the greatest influence on our own parenting styles is the way in which we were parented in our family of origin.

The Parents' Relationship

Assess the degree and nature of any conflict in the parents' own relationship. Due to the sensitivity of the issue, it can be useful to approach it in terms of the impact the reported child problems have on the relationship. For example:

> **Difficult child behaviour can put a lot of strain on the parents' own relationship. Have you been having any problems in the way you get along?**

The Child's Relationships With Siblings and Significant Others

Enquire into the degree and nature of any conflict in the child's relationships with their siblings. When working with step-families, it is also important to enquire about the child's relationship with the parent who lives elsewhere. This is also the appropriate point at which to assess the child's relationships with relatives involved in the care of the child.

Financial and Environmental Stressors

Enquire into the impact of any financial difficulties on the family's living circumstances, as well as potential problems related to the family's living environment. For example:

> Are you having any financial difficulties at the moment that might be causing stress or making it difficult to make ends meet?
>
> Do you have any trouble with neighbours or problems with crime in your area?

Family History of Mental Illness

Enquire about occurrences of psychiatric disturbance in the extended family of the referred child. For example:

> Do either of you have relatives with a history of psychiatric problems?

CONTINUING ASSESSMENT

At the conclusion of the session, provide parents with a proposal for any further assessment procedures considered appropriate. Briefly describe any child assessment activities planned for the subsequent session, presenting a clear rationale for these plans. Finally, it is important that parents leave this session with knowledge of when they can expect to receive assessment feedback and discuss treatment options (this would typically be at the conclusion of the next session).

Session 2: Assessment of the Child and Parent–Child Interactions

Session 2

Major Components

- **ASSESSMENT OF CHILD GENERAL PRESENTATION AND ADJUSTMENT**
- **ASSESSMENT OF PARENT–CHILD INTERACTIONS**

A comprehensive psychological assessment of a child would involve checking their general presentation, health, and wellbeing; assessing cognitive/emotional state; and, if developmentally appropriate, interviewing the child for their views of the problem, school adjustment, and other problems parents might not know about. A comprehensive assessment will usually involve completion of selected self-report checklists, direct observation of parent–child or family interaction, self-monitoring procedures, and information-gathering from other clinicians and institutions who have contact with the child and family (for example, school, medical practitioner). It is not appropriate to cover these general aspects of child assessment in this manual. Rather, our role here is restricted to the general observational assessment process we use to characterise parent–child interactions of relevance to the treatment of the behavioural problems.

OBSERVATION OF FAMILY INTERACTION

Direct observations of behaviour as it occurs in its natural social context was a cornerstone of the early parent-training programs. However, their usefulness in modern clinical settings depends on the observation system employed, the nature of the behaviours of interest, the context within which they occur, and the resources available to the clinician. While the goals of direct observation will vary, in general they are to assess the type, frequency, duration, and intensity of problem behaviours; identify how parents provide immediate antecedents and consequences for the problem behaviours; assess the broader emotional tone of the parent–child relationship; and observe how family structures provide a context for the behaviours.

Given that an assessment session with the parents has already been conducted, the therapist will have a number of hypotheses that can be tested during the observation. Behaviours vary greatly, however, in their amenability to direct observation. Oppositional behaviour in young children (for example, crying, noncompliance, aggression) can be readily observed in the family home or clinic if the setting is selected appropriately. In the home, such behaviour tends to escalate at times when parents attempt to engage young children in routine activities such as bathing, bedtime, getting ready to leave on outings, and meal times (Sanders, Dadds, & Bor, 1989). In clinical settings, oppositional behaviour will similarly tend to occur when the parent tries to engage the child in structured teaching tasks or when compliance is enforced (for example, cleaning up toys).

Although many problem behaviours cannot be readily observed in clinical settings, a number of strategies have been developed for approximating naturally occurring parent–child interactions. Ideally, the procedure is designed to elicit the problem behaviours and observe the family interaction patterns in which they are embedded (Patterson & Reid, 1984). Further, this needs to be done in a way that best approximates the natural occurrence of these patterns and yet provides sufficient procedural structure to prevent conflict or aggression escalating to a level that may be unusually distressing for participants.

With young children, we use a semistructured parent–child interaction task in which parents are requested to engage in free independent play with their child and then lead their child through a number of structured activities. The typical procedure we use is:

- free play – parent and child
- drawing task – ask the parent to lead the child through some writing and drawing tasks
- novel adult and separation from parent – the observer joins in to play and after a short time asks the parent to leave for a short ime
- clean up – the parent returns, and joins with the child to clean up toys.

The observer can make qualitative observations of both the parents' and child's behaviour, as well as use more formal coding procedures, such as the Family Observation Schedule (Waugh & Sanders, 1993) for coding parent–child interactions where objective research data are required. Where the goal is to sample the immediate antecedents and consequences of child behaviour in a short time period, such structure is warranted in that it deliberately directs the parent to interact with the child. Where the clinician is more interested in the natural topography of parent–child interaction, less structure can be useful in providing data on the extent to which the parent structures activities for the child, provides routine, and gives attention.

As children approach middle childhood and adolescence, they become far more conscious of an observer's presence and are less likely to engage in open conflict with parents and siblings. With older children it is more important to provide structured guidelines or select settings that tend to prompt family interaction. Examples of such settings are family mealtimes and family meetings when current problems are opened up for general discussion and potential problem-solving. Similarly, where problem behaviours are secretive (stealing, truancy, sexual problems) or very low in frequency, direct observation of natural interactions are less likely to provide any useful data, and clinic-based family tasks or sole use of self-report may need to be employed.

A useful procedure that is now commonly used in clinical research into marital distress, parent–adolescent conflict, and family factors in severe psychopathology is the family problem-solving discussion. Such discussions are appropriate for children who are approximately seven to eight years and older. A wealth of research emphasises the role of problem-solving competence in protecting a family against conflict and breakdown. The major points for observation are the extent to which family members actively listen to each other's point of view, take time to agree on a problem definition, and generate solutions and action strategies or, conversely, interrupt each other, criticise, talk tangentially, and prevent problem-solving through vagueness, concreteness, and expression of hopelessness and despair.

Such a procedure has the potential to be stressful for family members. Clinicians need to be alert to the possibility of the discussion degenerating into a parent doing all the talking, lecturing, or criticising an overwhelmed child. While this provides an insight into an obvious parent–child problem, it should be terminated as quickly as practicable. The likelihood of this occurring is reduced somewhat, but not eliminated, by giving clear, simple instructions to the family about the importance of trying to find solutions to the problems, keeping the discussions to between 5 to 10 minutes and using problems nominated by the child as well as by the parent. The Issues Checklist (Robin, 1981) can be used to generate problems for discussion and is filled out by both parents and child. We use 5 to 10 minutes for discussion of the child's nominated problem, and a similar period for that of the parents.

ASSESSMENT FEEDBACK AND TREATMENT PROPOSAL

The end of this assessment session can be an appropriate time to present assessment feedback and discuss treatment options, provided that the child is able to wait in another room. Meeting with parents only, present a summary of the assessment findings, including feedback of available diagnostic and prognostic information. The discussion of treatment options should follow, and include a proposal of treatment duration and contact frequency or, if necessary, further assessment procedures. Just as important as the content of this feedback is the process of encouraging a positive attitude in parents towards actively confronting the identified problems. The following is an example of the detail of diagnostic and prognostic feedback appropriate at this point in the interview:

> You can imagine that here at a psychology clinic we see all sorts of children, and they all vary in terms of the severity of their problems. Aaron is displaying moderate oppositional behaviour, which can be very difficult to parent. He really knows how to push your buttons by not following instructions, back-chatting, and so on. He's also clumsy with other children and a little pushy and aggressive, but this seems to be less of a problem. Nevertheless, it can mean that he may be on a pathway that may cause him some problems when he's further into school. The bad news about conduct problems is that, left untreated, they can get worse over time, until as an adolescent the child has real problems. So, you have both done really well by deciding to do something about it now.
>
> We've also spoken about various family issues, which we always assess because they're so important. A lot of the families we see are falling to pieces, and what I see in front of me here is two loving and competent parents doing a good job. Nevertheless, you've mentioned that you feel some disapproval from your own parents about the way you're parenting Aaron, and that puts you in a tense situation and can make you feel very emotional.
>
> Now, regarding Aaron's behaviour, it could get worse if you just let it go, but the good news is that we have a program for treating these behaviours that can improve things fairly quickly. The treatment of choice for this problem is for the three of us to go through some strategies – 'super-parenting' strategies – so that you, the parents, become therapists to help a little boy like Aaron control his emotions, and become more cooperative.

The therapist should be focused on ensuring that parents leave this assessment interview ready to participate fully in the skills-focused sessions to follow. The first step here is to invite parents to express their views on the proposed approach to treatment. If the expectations of parents appear incongruent with such a model (for example, insisting that therapists deal directly with the child, denying that their parenting practices can be improved), such ideas should be addressed directly in a non-confrontational manner.

It can be useful to address a number of assumptions associated with the parent-training model, pre-empting the concerns commonly expressed by parents in response to the parent-training material.

Session 2

Points that can be made include:

- Even though the focus is on ways parents should act with their child, this does not necessarily mean that they are presently doing anything wrong, as different approaches work with different children.
- Some of the ideas presented will be things the parent may be familiar with, and may already be doing. However, depending on how these strategies are used, they can have little effect, or even exacerbate problem behaviours.
- Treatment sessions will focus on implementing these strategies in a way that creates the maximum change in the child's behaviour. The process of therapy is therefore one of fine-tuning these strategies.

Once a shared perception has been developed and parents are enthusiastic about the proposed treatment, every attempt should be made to inspire optimism, enthusiasm, and a preparedness to work hard in the sessions to come. In doing this, the therapist can act as the 'coach', even making statements that may seem more appropriate to athletes or sportspeople. This is also a good chance to inject some humour. For example:

> Next week, we will have a session with you and your child to conduct a direct observation of your child and their behaviour. After that, we should be ready to get into the treatment. Be prepared to work hard at that session – the more you put in, the more you will see a change in [child's name]'s behaviour. The more effort you put in at this beginning stage, the less you will have to put in for the long term. So, get plenty of sleep before the next session and have your tracksuits on for a work-out!

Session 3: Strategies

Major Components

- **PRESENT THE ATTENTION/ATTACHMENT MODEL OF CONDUCT PROBLEMS**
- **INTRODUCE ATTACHMENT-RICH POSITIVE REINFORCEMENT STRATEGIES AND ATTACHMENT-NEUTRAL DISCIPLINE STRATEGY**
- **MATERIALS FOR SESSION**

It is important to note that we advocate combining the reward and discipline strategies into a single extended session. This differs from many BFI programs where it is typical to split this into two sessions, one devoted to reward strategies and one to discipline. The reason we try to combine them into one is for maximum impact value; that is, we ask parents to begin to implement all the major strategies at once on a pre-planned day when the new program has a good chance of working (that is, not on a day when the extended family drops by for a visit, or one parent is out of town!).

It is difficult for parents to implement a complete shift in attention and attachment balance (that is, from misbehaviour to positive behaviour) if they do not know what to do when the child misbehaves. Our experience is that many parents who have first received training only in reward strategies start off with the rewards and get some immediate success, but find themselves at a loss when and if the child engages in problem behaviour. They return the next session feeling discouraged and the program has lost a little of its momentum and credibility. Thus, we try to train all the techniques in one extended session. Although this is a lot for parents for take in, we believe it is better to give the complementary reward and discipline strategies together.

This is because the social learning and attachments aspects of all BFI programs are about the balance of attention to positive versus negative child behaviour. They are not about any one technique; the goal is to maximise attachment-rich attention to positive child behaviour and make responses to misbehaviour minimal, predictable, boring, and attachment-neutral.

Given that this is a great deal of information for the therapist to present and the parent to take in, we leave Session 4 relatively open. Thus, therapists who find the amount of material in Session 3 onerous can present the discipline strategies in this session and the reward strategies in the next. Therapists who can comfortably present all the material in the session and find that they have additional time can use that time to review and finetune implementation of the strategies.

The relevant handouts in the appendices at the back of this book are to be photocopied and handed out at the beginning of the session.

WELCOME AND AGENDA

At the beginning of every session, invite parents to describe any significant events/changes that may have occurred since the previous contact. When presenting details of a child's behaviour, parents may refer to a range of behaviours, suggesting that these represent diverse and discrete problems. Parents can be helped to feel less overwhelmed if such behaviours are summarised in terms of common features. For example, it may become apparent that child behaviours such as refusing to shower, failing to pick up clothes, and neglecting allocated chores all involve the same reinforcement traps. However, at this stage only basic commonalities should be identified, such as non-compliance with instructions. Alternatively, parents may report dramatic improvements in their child's behaviour following the initial assessment session. Such reports are often the result of increased optimism related to the commencement of treatment, and should be interpreted with caution.

Example of the agenda for Session 3:

> **Today we will cover two major parts. First, I'd like to talk about why these problems have developed in [child's name], and in doing so I'd like to share ways of understanding this behaviour. The ideas we talk about are going to form the entire basis for the action we take, and are just as important as the techniques you'll be using. The second major part will be on the actual techniques you'll be using, and how to use them to maximise improvements in your child.**

PSYCHOEDUCATION: THE CAUSES OF CHILD BEHAVIOUR

In this component parents are engaged in a guided discussion of factors potentially implicated in the aetiology and maintenance of their child's behaviour problems. When introducing this exercise, emphasise that parents know their child better than anyone else. Throughout the process, listen to the ideas contributed by parents, and respond to them in a way that identifies them as valid within the scientific framework being presented to them.

Explain to parents that the research on which child psychology is based has identified a number of factors that commonly contribute to oppositional behaviour in children. Explain that these different factors will be discussed separately, during which time parents should be asking themselves how the respective factors might apply to their child and family. After each factor has been discussed, parents will be asked to add any ideas they think might be important in understanding their child's behaviour. It should be emphasised that the aim is to reach an agreement about the problem and its causes, which will form the basis for the treatment provided. This exercise works well if parents are given the relevant handout to look at while discussing the respective material.

For each group of factors, a number of key points should be emphasised:

GENETICS AND BIOLOGY

- Child temperament/personality traits are relatively stable over time (that is, a person exhibiting impulsivity/inhibition/high activity levels as a child is likely to exhibit similar attributes as an adult).
- In themselves, such traits are neither good or bad (that is, it is possible to have two children who resemble each other closely in their traits, yet differ markedly in their behaviour). Such traits are therefore only part of the story.

PARENT–CHILD INTERACTIONS

- While each of these processes can be illustrated with very obvious examples, these factors (for example, accidental rewards for misbehaviour, ignoring desirable behaviour) often impact on child behaviour in a range of very subtle ways.
- Although it is important to understand how different parent–child interactions can influence child behaviour, such insight alone is often not sufficient to achieve meaningful change in child behaviour. Accordingly, the current program provides parents with a concrete plan for responses to difficult child behaviour.

THINGS AFFECTING PARENTS

- A child cannot feel settled if their parents do not also feel this way.
- In the current program it is considered important that attention is given to issues affecting broader parent and family wellbeing; however, it is advisable to begin by addressing child behaviour. Attention will be shifted to these areas once parents are in greater control of their child's behaviour.

Where possible, illustrate these factors with examples derived from material previously presented by the parent. After introducing and explaining each cluster, invite parents to suggest which factors they consider applicable to their child. Finally, ask parents if they can think of any remaining factors that may be important in understanding how the respective problem behaviours developed in their child.

Throughout this discussion, use language that reflects the tentativeness of the interpretations being made by the therapist or parent (for example, 'It appears that ...', or 'It may be possible that ...'). Conclude with a brief summary of the agreed-upon factors.

Explain to parents that the proposed treatment will target the second group of factors (parent–child interactions) and, where relevant, will address the third group (things affecting parents). However, the approach to treatment will be guided by factors such as child temperament in the first group (genetics and biology).

THE ROLE OF ATTENTION IN MAINTAINING OPPOSITIONAL BEHAVIOUR

Using Socratic questioning, facilitate a discussion illustrating the role of parental attention in the maintenance of oppositional child behaviours.

Introduction:

> The essence of this program is based on attention, and I want to start by giving you an example of this. Imagine this scenario. You're in the kitchen in the afternoon preparing dinner, and the children are elsewhere in the house ... and everything is quiet.

Prompt parents with the following questions. Typical parent responses are included in brackets. If parents fail to offer such responses after some prompting, acknowledge and praise their response, then provide the desired answer and check for adequate understanding.

- So what are you going to do in that situation?

(Sneak up and see what they're doing;

Ignore and get on with own business.)

- Why are you sneaking up to have a look?

(for example, Catch child misbehaving; Avoid interrupting child if not misbehaving)

- What if they're not doing anything wrong?

(for example, Offer some praise; Walk away)

- What would you do if you were in the kitchen, busy or relaxing, and you know that they're not doing anything wrong?

(Continue on, without getting involved in what they're doing.)

- If you stay in the kitchen and you don't go and get involved with them, what would happen sooner or later?

(for example, They might fight; Seek out parent)

Clarify the ideas illustrated in the scenario:

- Let's think about that story. It's very interesting because it reveals how we all act, and the things we do that can allow misbehaviour to develop.
- What happens when it's quiet? Well, first of all you usually think something is wrong, and as soon as you realise that nothing is wrong, you usually withdraw. You stay in the kitchen. What happens then is that they do something to get your attention, such as fight, or come to you. You'll deal with it, but as soon as you know that everything is okay again, you'll stay in the kitchen. Also, when we want to check on them, we often try to be unobtrusive.
- So, what happens is that you get into this trap, where for good behaviour there is very little engagement or attention, but for misbehaviour, they get incredible amounts of engagement/attention from you.
- Getting attention can be one of the main reasons children misbehave. It's very easy to get into a trap where a child misbehaves and it gets the parent engaged. Then, as soon as the child stops, we think 'Phewww ...', and go about doing what we were doing. This creates an attentional trap, where attention – in the child's eyes – becomes associated more and more with misbehaving, and less and less with being well-behaved.
- In situations where you *can't* give the child attention, like when you're getting ready in the morning, what happens? He starts doing really silly things so that you have to go and interact with him. For him, this behaviour works. It gets your attention. Now we might try and do the right thing by giving them praise when they're behaving well, but compare that – (quietly) 'Oh, that's really good' – with (loud and explosive with wild gestures) 'Look!!! I've had enough! Aahhh!'. You know how crazy we can get when we're upset.
- So, comparing these two things, he's thinking 'Gee, I like that second one. Look what happens when I push this button!'. This kind of behaviour can get us really emotional. What we're going to do is reverse that. We're going to take away all the attention that happens when he misbehaves, so you're making discipline boring and impersonal, and shifting all that attention to when he's behaving well.

Check that parents understand this explanation before moving to the following component.

EXPLAINING ATTACHMENT

Explain the role of attachment in maintaining child misbehaviour. For example:

> During the program, we'll be using the term 'attachment' to refer to the emotional bonds between you and [child's name]. In some situations these feelings of attachment can be very intense and emotional, especially in situations where you're displaying a lot of emotion. This means that even when a parent is displaying negative emotions or shouting, a whole range of attachment feelings can be triggered. When [child's name] experiences intense feelings of attachment with you, a deep part of him is feeling like he's the most important person in the world, because he's the focus of your emotions.
>
> There are two principles here that are very important to understanding child behaviour:
>
> First, the intense feelings of closeness that a child experiences in attachment-rich interactions can be caused by negative parent emotions just as easily as positive ones.
>
> Second, the need to experience these attachment feelings can be the most powerful influence on a child's behaviour. When children find something that produces those feelings they will do it again and again, as long as it is providing the attachment-rich experience.
>
> It's important to understand then, that by changing which behaviours are receiving your attention and emotional responses, we are changing those behaviours [child's name] will be engaging in to feel that intense closeness. Children are experts at working out what behaviour is going to lead to these attachment-rich interactions, and they will learn very quickly that it is now a different set of behaviours that is needed.
>
> The major goal of this part of the program then is to make a massive shift in your attention from negative to positive behaviour. We are going to take all the emotional attention that [child's name] gets for misbehaviour and move it across to positive behaviour. This will mean increasing attachment-rich interactions in response to child positive behaviour, while making discipline calm and boring, or attachment-neutral.

Session 3

IDENTIFYING DESIRED CHILD BEHAVIOURS

Explain that the first step of the process is to decide which child behaviours the parents would like to increase in frequency, and to list these in the first section of the respective parent handout.

Begin by asking parents:

> What would you like to see [child's name] doing more of?
>
> What behaviours would you like to see more often?

While it is important for the chosen behaviours to be relevant to the individual child and desired by the parents, the therapist should encourage parents to consider various behaviours commonly lacking in children with oppositional behaviour. These include following instructions, playing nicely/cooperatively, playing independently, speaking in a nice voice, and accepting 'no' for an answer.

The aim here is to produce a list of four or so precise child behaviours that are expressed in simple, clear language that a child could understand. If parents digress and begin discussing problem behaviours, remind them that positive behaviours are the topic for the moment. After settling on approximately four behaviours, check whether any significant ones have been neglected.

RESPONDING TO DESIRABLE CHILD BEHAVIOURS

Introduce the idea of actively attending to desirable behaviours. For example:

> **What we want to do is catch her doing these behaviours. This means walking about the house actively trying to catch your child being good.**

Emphasise that while the respective behaviours may be occurring infrequently, they will nevertheless be apparent at least occasionally. For example:

> **I want you to go around and try to spring her doing these behaviours. These behaviours are all occurring, even in the naughtiest children. All children follow some instructions, and sometimes use a nice voice, and so on.**

ALTERNATIVE FORMS OF REWARD

Help parents generate methods for rewarding these behaviours through elaborating and modelling the techniques of (1) descriptive praise, (2) tangible rewards, (3) time with the child, and (4) physical affection, when each is suggested. Parents should note these rewards (and examples of each) in the boxes on the relevant handout.

Begin by asking parents:

> **What can you do when you notice these behaviours?**

The first response by most parents will be praise. Outline the specific method of descriptive praise, presenting a rationale and explaining how it differs from that which parents typically use. For example:

> **Descriptive praise involves describing the behaviour, not the child. This means that we are explicitly telling the child what it is that they are doing well. It is the opposite of non-specific praise, such as 'good boy' or 'well done'. This can be harder than it looks, because non-specific praise really comes naturally. It's very effective in increasing good behaviour though, because we're spelling out to the child exactly what it is that is getting our attention, and how they can get it in the future.**

The following guided discussion emphasises that in addition to praising the behaviour performed by the child, the praise should applaud the child's very compliance with the instruction or request:

1. Ask parents to suggest an example scenario in which they have instructed their child to perform some action.
2. Include this instruction or request in a statement such as:

> **Now imagine that you've told me to clean my room, and I've gone and done a little bit of it. What might you come and say to me?**

(Parents will often suggest some descriptive praise such as 'You're doing a great job putting your toys away', while forgetting to praise the child's actual compliance with the request.)

3. Acknowledge the parents' suggestions of praise and praise their responses.
4. Ask parents what else the child has done apart from cleaning their room (or whatever the request task involved). If the parents fail to identify that the child followed the instruction, offer a prompt such as:

   > You gave her an instruction to do it.

5. Emphasise that people typically forget to praise compliance itself. For example:

   > This is the one we never do. It just doesn't come naturally! Imagine if I ask her to bring me a pen or something, and she does it and I say: (blandly) 'Oh, thanks for doing that'. Now imagine she does it and I say: (warmly and excitedly) 'Hey Belinda, come here, you know what just happened then? I asked you to do something and you did it! Wooo hooo! This is you and me as a team! This is what we're after!'

Prompt parents to suggest other forms of rewards:

> Imagine she's in her room playing nicely with a friend or brother. What else could you go in there and do?

When parents identify one of the forms or reward, offer praise, and illustrate the use of such a reward in a brief example. For example:

> Great! You could give her something, and we'd call that a tangible reward. They can be good, not all the time, but you could go in there and say: 'You two are playing nicely together. Look here, I've brought you a special treat each'.

Provide prompts for more alternatives, listing those identified so far. For example:

> What else could you do? Praise, tangible rewards ... it's getting trickier now. What else can you do to show her that you're pleased?

If it is clear that the parents cannot think of more, present those outstanding, one by one, addressing each as above.

Address the importance of alternating different rewards. For example:

> Now, you've got four options here: praise, tangible rewards, time, and physical affection. The important thing to remember here is 'mix and match'. In other words, this is the part of parenting where you do *not* want to be consistent. You want to be erratic and all over the place. So, if the child follows an instruction, the first time you might go in there and say, 'You did what I asked you to do, I'm really proud of you'. The second time you might go in there and make a huge song and dance: 'We're all going down for an ice-cream! Belinda did exactly what she was told, I'm so proud of her'. The next time you might just give her a hug. You can reward the whole family for one person's behaviour. That's kind of nice as well.
>
> Constantly alter the way you're rewarding these behaviours. If you do respond in the same way each time, she'll just go, 'Oh, I think I'll just go back to pushing the old buttons and get them upset'. So, it's got to be unpredictable and emotional.

Recap the basic task. For example:

> Now, I want you to saturate this rewarding and praise on to good behaviour with Belinda, and anyone else in the family.

Check parents' understanding before proceeding.

UNWANTED REACTIONS TO REWARDS

'Planned ignoring' is introduced to parents as a means of managing the oppositional behaviours sometimes observed in children in reaction to a parent's use of praise or physical affection. Give parents an example of common oppositional responses to new rewards, and introduce the planned ignoring procedure. For example:

> Something to watch out for is that she might act really silly when you go in there and start doing this. If she's playing quietly in her room, and you go in there and say, 'Hey Belinda, great to see you playing so nicely', she might stick out her tongue at you. Now, don't go in there and respond to it. Just do what's called 'planned ignoring'. Just turn around and walk out. Just leave the room. Then, as soon as she's doing something nice again, go back and reward her again. If she does the same thing, just walk away again.

Explain that the child may require some time to become comfortable with different forms of reward. For example:

> If she doesn't like the hug at first, give her a bit of time to warm to it and start with another one.

Explain that the delivery of rewards should be unconditional in nature, not dependent on the child's active participation. For example:

> Children can get into a habit where they can do this thing to one parent. 'You're not welcome, I don't want to hug you'. So make sure that you're doing the praise at first for her. If you're going in there and saying, 'You've been really good, *give me* a hug', you're kind of making her have to give. So, start with a totally unconditional approach: 'I'm going to reward and give to you because you've been good'.

Summarise the anticipated difficulties, and the respective use of planned ignoring. For example:

> So remember, she may try to push you away at first. Don't respond to it. Often what happens is that you go like this, (frustrated) 'I don't believe this! I just wanted to ...', or something like that. Again, she thinks, 'Oohh! That really pushes Daddy's buttons. I can get him really emotional by doing that stuff'. So put her on planned ignoring, and put her on unconditional free gifts of praise. But don't let it discourage you. It actually means that she is trying to engage your attention, just in a way that's not very nice.

Check parents' understanding before proceeding.

ATTENTION TOP-UPS

Explain that if children have been playing independently, spontaneous praise from a parent may provoke attempts by the child to elicit further attention. Outline how this can be avoided by reinforcing periods of independent play using 'attention top-ups'. For example:

> The other common difficulty is that you might go in there and praise the children for playing nicely, and they think, 'Oh there's Mum, we don't want her to go', and they say, 'Don't go!' You really have to say, 'No, I am going, I have to prepare the meal, but see if you can keep playing'. Then try and go back before their attention span runs out and praise them again. So you're giving them the message, 'If you play nicely and quietly together, I'll come and praise you in little regular intervals, instead of you having to fight or come and seek me out'.

Check parents' understanding before proceeding.

ATTACHMENT-NEUTRAL RESPONSES TO MISBEHAVIOUR

The second set of child-management strategies involves a behaviour-correction routine that minimises attention to misbehaviour and uses a boring, predictable, and attachment-neutral approach. Conduct a role-play with parents, in which the therapist assumes the role of the child. The aim here is to present parents with the challenge of maintaining attachment neutrality when responding to misbehaviour.

Therapist:

> Imagine I'm your child and as I'm walking past you at the table you ask me to pass you a pen. Try to respond to me the way you might respond to your child.

Once the parent gives the request, the therapist (in the child role) then complies with the instruction.

Next, repeat the first scenario; however, when asked to pass the pen, the therapist this time walks past the table, ignoring the request and saying, 'Get stuffed'.

Ask parents to describe both of their responses. This is an interesting role-play because even though the parents have just been exposed to the ideas of reward, they will generally react much more intensely to the non-compliance than the compliance. The aim of the program is to make the response to the first act of compliance more powerful and attachment-rich than the response to the non-compliance.

Point out how these typical parent responses differ in the intensity of the attentional and attachment experience for the child. Ask parents to suggest how they could respond in each of these situations so that appropriate child behaviour is associated with an attachment-rich interaction and misbehaviour is followed by an attachment-neutral one.

This leads to the need for a simple behaviour-correction routine that is used to respond to misbehaviour. Explain how the same attention/attachment principle will be applied to misbehaviour. For example:

> What we're going to do now is the opposite of what you are doing when you praise the child for good behaviour. When you do that, you're being really emotional, really sing-songy. Now what I want you to do is, when she's misbehaving, be really boring. So, your voice goes down and becomes quiet and serious. It's just 'Kirsty, come here please'.

> When you hear effective teachers or disciplinarians, they always do this. Their normal talking voice is animated and emotional, and their discipline voice is boring, calm, and neutral.
>
> However, when you get tired or you get into a bad habit with children, you go to the opposite extreme. It's like this – (quiet and dull) 'Kirsty, today we're going shopping ... and we're ...' – and you talk in this monotone. Then, when they're misbehaving you start coming up – (volume escalates) 'I said, put that down!' It just builds up like that (upward sloping gesture with hand). So in other words, misbehaviour is affecting your emotional self-control.
>
> You've got to try to reverse that; discipline needs to be done very calmly and very quietly.

Check parents' understanding before proceeding.

Elicit the parents' typical responses to misbehaviour.

Here is a scenario:

> You're in the kitchen whipping up a pasta salad. She comes in, and she's in a bad mood. She stomps in and says, 'Yyyyyuck! I'm not going to eat that! I want a chocolate milk for dinner'.
>
> She says this in a very whiney, aggressive voice.

Ask:

> What would you usually do in that situation?

Elicit responses from both parents, and paraphrase in turn.

PRESENT THE STEPS FOR RESPONDING TO MISBEHAVIOUR

Introduce the component:

> OK, when she misbehaves, this is what I want you to do. Here are the steps.

STEP 1: GET THE CHILD'S ATTENTION

Emphasise the importance of first gaining the child's attention, and address practical issues relevant to this. For example:

> The first thing I want you to do is get her attention – this is really important. It doesn't matter what the misbehaviour is, you have to do this step.
>
> Even if you're standing at the bench working, and she comes in, I want you to do this: turn from where you're standing, walk over and bend down, as though placing your hands on child's upper arms.
>
> (Calm, quiet voice) 'Kirsty ...' – just get her attention – 'We're going to get very close, and very serious'. This is especially important if she's misbehaving somewhere else. There's no point in doing this: (cup mouth and shout) 'Kirsty! Leave your brother alone!'. Those instructions never work. Even though it's frustrating, it will save your energy in the long term. Go to her, bend down, and get her attention. It's so important. Your compliance rates are going to jump, simply by making the effort to go and do that.

Now, when you get close to her like that, she may turn her head or block her ears with her hands. Don't worry about that, because she can still hear you. Don't play that game – don't try and pull the hands away or anything, just get close and calmly say what you have to say. It's very important.

STEP 2: USE A 'CLARIFYING STATEMENT'

Describe the process of using what we call clarifying statements with children. For example:

> Then we're going to use what we call clarifying statements, which simply means that we're going to state the misbehaviour, and then say what the correct behaviour is. And that's what you do every time she misbehaves. You simply say what the misbehaviour is, then you say what she should do instead.

Model the procedure. For example:

> Imagine again that she has come into the kitchen and said, 'Eeewww, puke, I'm not eating that!'. What is it that she has done wrong here? It's the aggression voice. So you turn around (turn and bend down), and say, 'Kirsty, don't talk to me like that please. If you want something speak nicely'. Say what she shouldn't do, then what she should do.
>
> Imagine she comes into the kitchen and she's banging something. I'd say, 'Hey Kirsty, don't play with that at the moment please, I'd like you to just go outside and wait until dinner's ready'. If, for example, she's playing in a group and hits another child. The first thing you do is go up to her, get her attention, and say, 'Kirsty, I do not want any hitting or kicking towards other children. I want you to play nicely'.

Emphasise the need to minimise engagement and interaction with the child:

> The main thing we're trying to do here is to make it really calm and boring. If you talk, talk, talk, she's won again. When she comes in the kitchen and says, 'That's horrible! I'm not eating that!', and you say, 'Look! You're the child and I'm the parent ... this is what we're having for dinner and if you don't like it you can (ramble on) ...', this could go on for half an hour and she's got your total attention. So, you're trying to minimise talk.

The aim of the next guided dialogue is to allow parents to rehearse responding verbally to the current scenario using the clarifying-statement strategy. In the context of this initial attempt a number of common difficulties are explored, including child behaviour that conforms to the requested behaviour while implicating further challenges, and the frequent failure of parents to praise the very act of compliance.

Prompt parents with the following bulleted dialogue. Typical parent responses are included in brackets. If parents fail to offer such responses after some prompting, praise or acknowledge their response, provide the desired answer, and check that they understand. Say:

> Now let's talk about what to do if she complies. Go back to that scenario, and imagine this. You have gained her attention and calmly said to her, 'Kirsty, I want you to speak in a nice voice please'. Then she says, (in a calm voice) 'I don't like that. Can I have chocolate milk instead please?'.

Give parents time to consider the events described, then ask:

- Now, think carefully. What has she just done?

  (that is, the child followed instructions as requested)

- So, what are you going to do?

  (that is, praise her)

- What might you say here?

The praise suggested by parents is likely to neglect the child's actual act of compliance, requiring further prompting from the therapist. For example:

> That's very good – I think you're right on the money there. But, you praised her only for speaking nicely. She did more than that – it's something else on our list of desired behaviours.
>
> (that is, she followed instructions)
>
> Yes! It's so easy to forget this one.

Model the appropriate praise, including an appropriate response to the dilemma presented in the initial scenario. For example:

> 'Hey Kirsty! I just told you to speak in a nice voice, and you did! You're following instructions! Come here darling. Look, this is what dinner is, but we'll see about a chocolate milkshake or something afterwards.'

STEP 3: USE A 'FIRM INSTRUCTION'

Address the use of firm instructions following the failure of clarifying statements. For example:

> Now let's assume that she hasn't followed the instructions and starts to escalate her misbehaviour.

Ask parents to suggest some behaviours that their child may exhibit at times when they respond defiantly to instructions or discipline attempts. At such times a child may act with verbal or physical aggression. Parents often report provocative statements made by their child, such as, 'You're not the boss of me' or, 'I don't like you'. Explain that at times of such escalation, it is appropriate to use a firm instruction. Describe this process. For example:

> Okay, so her behaviour is escalating. What you do here is give a *firm instruction*. It's very similar to the clarifying statement. Say what not to do and say what to do. That's all it is. 'Kirsty, I want you to go outside the kitchen now and play nicely'. A really calm voice instruction like that. This instruction is the one that means last chance – 'This is the last time I'm speaking'.

STEP 4: USE TIME-OUT

Explain that if the child fails to comply following the use of a firm instruction, the next step is the use of time-out. For example:

> If she complies at this point, remember to respond with praise, the way we've been discussing it. However, if her behaviour continues to escalate, put her into time-out.

Check whether parents are currently using time-out, or have attempted it in the past.

Parents often report sources of conflicting information regarding the correct implementation of time-out (for example, whether to use the child's bedroom or a chair in the hallway), perhaps due to such widespread use of the strategy. Reassure parents that ultimately, the goal is to implement such strategies according to what works best for their child.

Present parents with the guidelines for choosing a space to function as the time-out area: (1) It needs to be a *safe* place, (2) It needs to be *boring*, and (3) it needs to be *neutral*.

Briefly summarise the use of the time-out. For example:

> We usually start with a bathroom or a spare room – neutral territory. That's time-out for all children in the family. It's a boring, neutral, dull environment – you have to go in there and just sit. It's also democratic in that all children in the family are placed in time-out for aggressive behaviour and deliberate rule-breaking.

SET UP A TIME-OUT REHEARSAL

Time-out should only be used after the child has seen it operate in playful rehearsal. Thus, at the start of the program, parents should set aside a time to show the child how it works. For young children we often suggest a role-play in which a child's teddy bear, or the family pet, or the father, pretends to misbehave. The parent shows the child how time-out works, with special attention to what happens if the child yells or breaks things in time-out (that is, time-out continues until quiet and calm), and what behaviours lead to time-out ending (two minutes being quiet and calm).

REVIEW THE BEHAVIOUR–CORRECTION ROUTINE STEPS

Clarify the timeframe within which the four-step sequence should be applied, emphasising the significance of this in the context of the strategy. For example:

> Now, see how we've just gone through this four-step sequence. This should take 15 seconds. Sometimes for you, like it is for most people, it's been taking an hour and a half to build up to that. That's often where the problem is.

Model the application of the four-step sequence. For example:

> Let me act out the whole thing. Ready?
>
> (Therapist stands and walks to the corner of the room.)
>
> You're in the kitchen (make cooking gestures), and she comes in, 'Eewww! Yuuuuck!'. (Therapist crouches down). 'Kirsty, come here for a second. Don't speak in that voice please, and if you want something speak nicely'.

> If she speaks nicely I'll praise her. However, if she gets aggressive, move to step three, and give one other firm instruction: 'Hey, speak to me nicely, and I'd like you to go outside and find something else to do.'
>
> Now, she may comply, but let's go to the worst-case scenario. She's now screaming or kicking (therapist acts out). I just say, 'Excuse me Kirsty, you haven't done as you were told. It's time-out please'.
>
> See? It's that quick. Now, she may go to time-out by herself, but she probably won't, so we just pick the child up and carry her quietly to the time-out area. Then we say, 'When you've been quiet for two minutes (or whatever short period) you can come out'.

It is common at this point for parents to state that such an approach might be impractical either at some particular time, or in some setting. Ask for permission to address these concerns following the current discussion of the general strategy.

Check that parents understand the process demonstrated.

Review the rationale for the approach, addressing the levels of emotion and impact associated with the ways in which parents typically respond to desired behaviour and misbehaviour respectively. For example:

> Now, let's review why these strategies are effective. It's important to understand that you can do all of this and it won't work if you do not get the balance correct; that is, the reward strategies are quiet and bland and boring – attachment-neutral – and less important to the child than the responses they can get for misbehaviour. The program also sometimes doesn't work because the discipline process and time-out are presented with anger and rejection – that is, only used after the misbehaviour has escalated into attachment-rich zones.
>
> The balance has to be reversed. That's why these programs work. The child should realise, 'Oh wow! I can get all the passion and the attention I need from Mum and Dad through niceness rather than evil' (humour!).

Discuss the likelihood of a rebound effect when first introducing the strategies discussed this session. For example:

> Just a final warning – when you first start putting these strategies into practice, your child is going to notice that things are different, and that he's not getting the same reactions and attention that he is used to. After he becomes familiar with these strategies, he'll learn that he's no longer able to get exciting attention and big displays of emotion through misbehaviour. However, before he learns this, he'll probably try his best to get those same old reactions out of you, and he will do this by making his behaviour even worse. This is normal, and doesn't last very long. The most important thing is to keep going with it.

Present parents with a summary of the messages implicit in the use of the respective child-management strategies with their child. For example:

> So, the message that you're giving [child's name] by doing these things is this: 'You're a lovely little girl, and we're a happy family. I'm going to catch you being good, and I'm going to praise you. I love you, and I'm going to show it all the time. But, as soon as there is any misbehaviour, instead of getting all upset, it's going to be boring and fast and over in 10 seconds. Then we'll try and get back to the good side of things'.

CONCLUDING COMMENTS

As this is the first session in which the parents have been presented with specific strategies, it can be useful to address the overall process of putting everything into practice. Summarise the main points:

- Catch your children behaving well and get excited about it.
- Use a range of reward strategies, especially focusing on the most difficult one, giving your time to the child. Be unpredictable.
- Respond to misbehaviour with minimal talk and a boring, predictable, attachment-neutral discipline strategy.
- It is all about balance – 'time-in' is much more appealing than 'time-out'.

Remind parents not to start until they have rehearsed the child strategies and have everything in place ready to go and free from disruptions.

Session
3

Session 4: Continue–Review–Finetune

Major Component

■ **CONTINUATION OR REVIEW OF PREVIOUS SESSION**

Regardless of a therapist's skill in introducing the behavioural strategies of the previous session, the correct or optimal implementation of these strategies by parents cannot be assumed. The task of reviewing parents' first week of implementation is critical to the success of the treatment, and demands great attention to process. This session requires flexibility and creativity on the part of the therapist, with methods such as impromptu role-plays that are useful in revealing important details of the parent–child interactions reported by parents. Most importantly, however, an effective review requires a therapeutic alliance in which parents feel comfortable disclosing difficulties experienced when attempting to implement these strategies, openly discussing issues that may be impacting upon this implementation, and hearing constructive criticism regarding their efforts.

REVIEWING REWARD IMPLEMENTATION

1. Ask parents to indicate how often they were able use the reward strategies in the previous week.
2. Ask parents to give examples of the *behaviours* they rewarded, and the *rewards* they used (for example, ask parents to repeat their exact words when using praise, and so on).
3. Throughout this process help the parents to identify difficulties that limited their use of these strategies.
4. Where appropriate, address the three areas below.

REVIEW OF THE GOOD BEHAVIOURS CHOSEN IN THE PREVIOUS SESSION

It is common for parents to report having given generous rewards for child inactivity (for example, praising the child for simply being quiet), while neglecting to focus on actual positive behaviours (for example, speaking in an appropriate voice, following instructions, and so on). Make an effort to focus the parent's attention on the specific behaviours they chose to encourage in the previous session. Ask parents to recall these behaviours and discuss their opportunities to reward each of these. Addressing each of these in turn, praise the efforts of parents while helping them to identify ways in which they might reward each of these behaviours more intensely.

REVIEW OF THE DIFFERENT TASKS OF REWARDING GOOD BEHAVIOURS

Relevant tasks include:

- attending to good behaviour (that is, noticing when the behaviours actually occur)
- using descriptive praise and remembering to praise actual compliance (for example, 'Hey Neville, you did exactly what I asked you to do!')
- delivering rewards in an attachment-rich manner (for example, being emotional and animated)
- using a variety of rewards (and alternating these)
- using planned ignoring in response to a child's unwanted reactions to rewards.

Ask parents about each of these.

CREATING OPPORTUNITIES TO REWARD GOOD BEHAVIOUR

The following issues are important to address when parents report limited (or nil) opportunities to reward particular child behaviours.

Explain to parents that we can *create* these opportunities. This involves setting up situations in which it is *easier* for the child to perform various desirable behaviours.

Emphasise that by helping children to perform very basic desirable behaviours, parents can then build on these behaviours until they generalise to the kind of desirable behaviour that is developmentally appropriate. For example:

> Children usually have a range of 'high-risk' instructions that they hardly ever comply with (for example, 'Please get ready for you bath'). There will also be a set of easier instructions that the child complies with more reliably (for example, 'Please get the cordial bottle out of the fridge'). When we need to, we can throw the child some these easy instructions. As soon as we see anything that remotely resembles the good behaviour we want, we have the opportunity to build on it until it spills over into situations in which it is harder for the child to behave well. It's like you're 'getting your foot in the door' with the child's good behaviour.

ADVANCED REWARD STRATEGIES

The aim of this component is to present additional reward strategies that may be of use to the family in question. These are strategies that are not included routinely, yet may be useful in some circumstances. Indications for each strategy are presented below:

PLANNED CHILD-CENTRED TIME

Children who are most likely to benefit from planned child-centred time are those lacking routine and/or individual attention from a parent or caregiver. The strategy involves parents allocating regular time periods for the purpose of engaging the child in child-directed play.

Introduce the component, and present a brief rationale. The following points are relevant to include:

- The basic idea of the strategy is to give your child attention when you are able to, so they do not demand it when you are not.
- The strategy gives parents an opportunity to reward appropriate behaviours.

- The strategy provides a positive, relationship-enhancing experience for both the parent and child. The child feels that they are special, and reciprocates with warmth. The parent and child accordingly feel closer.
- There are no specific time requirements; however, from 15 to 30 minutes is an appropriate period of time. The most important thing is to do it every day.
- It will work best if you use the strategy with all children in the family.

Discuss the role of the parent during such periods, including the following points:

- When being child-centred/child-focused, the parent should allow the child to make decisions related to the play (for example, the activity/game played).
- Instead of giving the child instructions, the parent should simply show interest in what the child is doing by asking the child questions and presenting observations about the actions of the child.

Address practical issues relevant to implementing planned child-centred time.

Finding Time

For example:

> One of the hardest things about undertaking planned child-centred time is finding a regular time that's available for this purpose. When you're first starting to use this, it can be a case of trying it at different times and seeing what time best suits. It's also important to plan ahead and work out if other commitments need to be reorganised.

If parents exhibit hesitation about deciding on a particular time at which to attempt the strategy, encourage them to utilise a problem-solving approach. For example:

> It can be useful to list a few different times of the day that might be appropriate. Then work out (1) what things might make it hard to do it at those times, and (2) what different steps could be taken to address the things preventing you from using those times.

The Child Becomes Disruptive

For example:

> It's possible that at times [child's name] will start to get a little disruptive or difficult during these play sessions. If this happens, and the child doesn't respond to requests to behave, simply leave him to play alone.

Siblings Interfere

For example:

> If it gets difficult to give [child's name] individual attention because his brother or sister tries to disrupt this special time, there are a few ways to deal with it. Explain to them that this is your special time with [child's name], and that you will soon be doing the same for the sibling. If the sibling does not respond, reschedule the child-centred play for a time when the sibling is occupied with some other activity (for example, during their favourite TV show; while they're eating afternoon tea).

Model the role of the parent during child-centred time, and engage the parents in a role-play of the strategies involved (for example, praising appropriate behaviour, making observations and asking questions about the actions of the child, and so on).

REVIEW BEHAVIOUR-CORRECTION PROCEDURES

1. Determine how active the parent has been in responding to the respective behaviours (that is, how often and how much time was spent engaged in the implementation of the proposed activities).
2. Invite parents to comment on what they believe they did well, and praise appropriate efforts.
3. Invite parents to comment on what they found to be the most difficult aspects of the procedures. Encourage clients to reflect on why these problems occurred and, if appropriate, problem-solve with the client.
4. Praise the client for reporting any difficulties, emphasising that addressing such problems collaboratively as soon as they occur ensures that treatment gains will be maximised.
5. If parents have been using the respective strategies in a restricted way (intentionally or otherwise), discuss ways the parent might generalise their use of the strategies.
6. Collaboratively problem-solve any difficulties with implementation and set precise strategies for fine-tuning implementation.

MAKING ADJUSTMENTS TO TIME-OUT

The purpose of this component is to address the flexibility that can be applied to the time-out strategy. For most children with significant oppositional behaviour, it is apparent that time-out is an appropriate course of action. However, once a child demonstrates improved compliance during the procedure, it may no longer be necessary to implement the process with the same restrictions.

Introduce this issue and discuss the associated options. For example:

> Most children with difficult behaviour often reach a point where time-out is the only thing that will calm them down. However, once a child becomes familiar with time-out and starts showing that they are becoming more cooperative, it's a good idea to tone it down a little. We can do this by reducing time-out down to what we call 'quiet time'.

Explain the quiet-time procedure. For example:

> Remember that this is simply an adjustment to the time-out step of the behaviour-correction routine, so everything that comes before it will stay the same. We'll speak about how to explain it to children in a moment, but they don't need to know that we call it something different, so you'll still be saying, 'You've done the wrong thing, you need to go to time-out'. Then, immediately guide the child to the quiet-time area, which can be a chair in a hallway or in the corner of a room.
>
> Then, just like in time-out, say something like, 'After you've sat here quietly for two minutes you can come back'. Don't speak to your child, and make sure that other people stay away. If the child gets too disruptive or keeps trying to get out of the chair, then put them into full time-out for another two minutes. Then, just as with time-out, when they come out, engage them in some activity and catch them being good.

Address the process of implementing changes to time-out. For example:

> Before you begin making changes to time-out, you need to explain things to your child. Don't wait until there's a problem, find a time when everything is fine, and explain that the child has been doing time-out really well, and has stopped making a lot of noise or trying to escape from the time-out area. Then explain that because of these improvements, you'll be using a chair out in the open rather than a closed-in time-out area.

HOMEWORK

- Continue to implement the reward and discipline procedures, and incorporate child-centred time.
- Implement the suggested solutions to any difficulties identified and discussed.

GOAL-SETTING

Summarise the progress achieved so far, and the difficulties reported by parents. Collaboratively negotiate short goals for improving the implementation of the reward and discipline strategies. Devise a concrete plan of the steps parents can take to achieve these goals, and discuss/problem-solve any issues that may impact on this process.

Session
4

Session 5: Contextual Issues

Major Components

- **FIGHTING WITH SIBLINGS**
- **BOREDOM-BUSTERS/HIGH-RISK SETTINGS**
- **FAMILY RULES**
- **MATERIALS FOR SESSION**

This session introduces other strategies for child management that complement the basic reward/discipline program. The need for each of these will vary from family to family; however, we find their use so important that we include them routinely.

The relevant handouts in the appendices at the back of this manual are to be photocopied and handed out at the beginning of the session.

MANAGING SIBLING CONFLICT

Introduce the component and present a basic rationale for the strategies to follow. For example:

> All siblings argue from time to time. However, it becomes a problem when it occurs regularly and/or becomes severe in terms of potential hurt. Most arguments between siblings occur as a way of getting you involved. Therefore, it commonly occurs at times when you are present but occupied elsewhere (working, with visitors, in the kitchen, on the telephone, and so on).

Present the strategies for reducing sibling conflict:

FOSTER POSITIVE PLAY

- Reward cooperative play and sharing.
- Reward periods of *non*-fighting.
- Make sure both children are rewarded as a team.
- Spend time with each child individually (special time) and as a pair.
- Reward children for coming and telling you about nice, shared activities.

DEAL EFFECTIVELY WITH ARGUING

- Try not to listen to tittle-tattle.
- Minimise refereeing – if an argument needs to be stopped, apply blame equally between the children. There is no point in trying to figure out who started it.

- When fighting occurs and the parent must intervene, the children should be disciplined as a pair, generally by either separating the children for a brief period or removing the object of the argument for a short period (for example, TV, a toy).
- If arguing persists, separate the children by specifying activities and locations that are apart for a specified period.

BOREDOM-BUSTERS AND HIGH-RISK SITUATIONS

Introduce boredom-busters and provide a brief rationale. For the steps involved in implementing boredom-busters, see the corresponding parent handout.

Explain that for all children there are particular situations in which they are much more likely to misbehave. Tell parents that the following component will address the management of behaviour in such high-risk settings. For example:

> All children have particular situations in which it seems much harder for them to behave; they're much more likely to really act up, and are often harder to control. We're now going to talk about how to manage these high-risk settings.

Review the situations in which the child's behaviour is most problematic for the parents, as obtained in the assessment interview.

Briefly discuss these situations with the parents, exploring what such settings might be like for a child hungry for stimulation and engagement. Address the extent to which parent–child interaction is possible during the respective situations.

Choose one of these situations, and ask the parents:

> I would like you to each take a moment to put yourself in [child's name] shoes, and imagine that you're being driven in the car by Mum or Dad. Now, I want you to imagine what this is like for a child who is hungry for stimulation and attention. What would this be like? What might the child be thinking?

If the parents fail to suggest that the child would be bored, prompt such a response. Summarise this response and explain that disruptive behaviour in such situations is often due to a lack of engagement. For example:

> She's probably going to be feeling pretty bored. And this is something that seems to characterise these situations where children are much more likely to misbehave. In these high-risk settings the child is bored and lacking engagement.

Ask the parents to consider the restrictions placed upon their capacity to occupy their child in the respective situation. For example:

> Now have a think about the things that you are usually doing in that situation. When you are doing these things is it possible for you to interact with [child's name] in the way that you usually do? Why not?

Summarise the parent's response, recognising the genuine limitations imposed on the parent's capacity to engage with the child in the situation. Explain that in such high-risk settings it is often not possible for parents to occupy their child because they themselves are required to focus substantial attention on some other task. For example:

When you're driving it's obviously very difficult to give [child's name] the same kind of attention you can in other situations, because you need to attend to the road. Usually in the situations where children are much more likely to misbehave there are very real restrictions in the way a parent can interact with their child. So, the child is bored and hungry for engagement, but there's not much that the parent can do about it at the time.

Briefly outline the concepts underlying the use of boredom-busters. For example:

The approach we use in these kinds of situations involves what we call 'boredom-busters', and it's designed to overcome this problem. It involves getting the child absorbed in some activity that will hold their attention so that they're so engaged in what they're doing that they don't get bored and look for attention by misbehaving.

This is based on the principle that *prevention is better than cure*. In these situations, because the child's behaviour is so excessive, it can often be quite difficult to take control after they have started to act up and, as we've discussed, you are often restricted in how you can interact with the child. But, by doing a little bit of planning ahead we can avoid the disruptive behaviour we usually see at such times. It's basically about doing a little bit when it's easiest to get through to the child, rather than having to do a lot of work during the situation, when it's much harder to get through to them.

IMPLEMENTING BOREDOM-BUSTERS

Restate the aim of boredom-busters. For example:

The thing to remember with boredom-busters is that anything that keeps a child occupied, busy, or engaged is going to decrease the likelihood that they will be disruptive and demand attention.

Explain the first step of identifying available options to engage the child. For example:

The first task then is to work out what you can do that will accomplish these things effectively. These need to be things that the child can become involved with independently, and that are appropriate for the setting you're about to go into.

Facilitate the parent in generating alternative methods for occupying the child, continuing with the example high-risk setting discussed earlier.

Begin by asking:

We've just been talking about what happens when you need to drive with her for long periods. Let's brainstorm the things that could be used to occupy her in settings like this.

The final list should include the following:

- assigning pertinent tasks to the child (for example, during a shopping trip, providing the child with a list of things to help the parent locate while shopping)
- assigning arbitrary tasks to the child (for example, during a long car trip home, asking the child to draw a picture of their favourite part of the day)
- self-contained games (for example, travel board games, hand-held computer games)

- games involving intermittent interaction (for example, I spy).

> Such tasks, whether pertinent or arbitrary, can be made even more effective by incorporating appropriate rewards.

When parents identify an appropriate method, offer praise, and illustrate the use of the method using a relevant scenario.

Provide prompts for more alternatives, encouraging the parents to be creative. For example:

> What else could you do to hold her attention? This is one of the times when creative parenting is required. Remember that you know your child better than anyone else, so you're the best authority on things that could keep her busy.

If it is clear that parents cannot think of any more alternatives, present any outstanding methods, addressing each as above.

Move on to the second step; that is, preparing the child for the situation. For example:

> The next step is to talk to the child about the situation before you go into it. It's really important to do this when you're using these boredom-busters. If you need to change some part of your routine to accommodate this, such as getting ready 10 minutes earlier, it's important that you do. You need to get the child's attention and calmly explain the problems that have occurred previously in the situation. Then, prompt the child to describe how they should behave in the situation. Be sure to praise appropriate suggestions made by the child, and summarise these in terms of rules. Depending on the method you're going to use to occupy the child, it may be appropriate to also tell them what you have planned for them. Finally, make sure that you have easy access to any materials you might need (for example, colouring books, pencils, and so on).

Describe approaches to facilitating the child's engagement in activities, explaining that children may not become immersed in activities simply because they are available. Parents are presented with three approaches for maintaining a child's involvement in an activity: praise, novelty, and joining in with the child.

USE OF PRAISE

For example:

> The first thing we can do is use an approach that we have been using in a whole lot of different ways – praise. You can use the same descriptive praise that you have been using for all of the behaviours that you want to increase.

USE OF NOVELTY

For example:

> Something else we can do to maintain a child's involvement is to make use of what we know about novelty. Children are likely to show more interest in new things than in things that they do all the time. The way we make use of this is not by buying the child a new toy every time they get bored, but making sure that you have a variety of activities available, and that you move on to new ones before the child becomes bored with the current one – before their attention span runs out.

JOINING IN WITH THE CHILD

For example:

> Another really effective way to increase and maintain a child's interest in an activity is for us to show interest in what they're doing. The way we do this is by letting the child lead the way, responding with interest to any initiation or comment that they might make. This involves answering questions asked by the child, asking questions about what the child is doing, and praising the child where appropriate.

PROVIDING CHILDREN WITH FEEDBACK ABOUT THEIR BEHAVIOUR

Following the discussion of these approaches, model the process for providing children with constructive feedback about their behaviour following an event in a high-risk setting. In the role of the parent, the therapist feedback pertaining to both desired and undesired behaviours performed by a child during some event.

FAMILY RULES

ESTABLISHING FAMILY RULES

Explain the use and purpose of family rules. For example:

> With the approaches we have been looking at so far, part of the way you respond to misbehaviour is to tell the child the correct behaviour they should be doing. Another useful way to give children a clear idea about how they should behave is to have a set of ground rules. These are rules that you decide in advance about the way family members need to behave. They can be particularly useful for problem behaviours that recur over and over. They can also be used for particular situations; so, you might have a set of ground rules for when people are visiting, or for when you're having some personal time to yourself.

Explain the process for establishing family rules. For example:

> Ground rules work best when you follow a few guidelines. We want to keep it simple, so only have a small number of rules. These should be easy for the child to follow, as well as be easy for you to enforce. For example, they need to be specific enough to be able to tell when a child is or is not following them. It's also important that the rules apply to all the children in the family so they are fair to everyone.
>
> When you have decided on some rules, it's important that they are stated in positive terms, describing what the child can do, rather than what they are forbidden from doing. For example, 'A quiet voice must be used inside the house' rather than, 'No yelling inside the house'.
>
> Finally, before you can introduce the rules to your family, you need to have decided how you will manage the violation of different rules. This may involve time-out, or the use of what we call 'logical consequences'.
>
> Logical consequences are basically punishments that relate directly to the problem that's occurring. For example, if you have a ground rule that states, 'Children must turn off the television when asked by a parent', a logical consequence for failing to do this might be forbidding the child from watching TV

for the next hour. However, it's important to make sure that such consequences are not excessive. For example, if the TV were withdrawn for too long, the child would just feel like giving up.

Explain the process for introducing family rules. For example:

Choose a time when there are no distractions so the child can concentrate on what you are talking about, and explain that you have got something new that you would like to tell them about.

First, describe what you are going to be doing and why. For example, 'We thought it would be a good idea to work out what the house rules are, so that everyone knows what they need to do, and it's fair for everyone'. For each rule, state it clearly, and check that the child understands it. You also want to show that you are interested in their ideas about the rule, so ask your child what they think about it. Then, to make sure that the child has understood, ask them to repeat the rule back to you. Finally, recap the list of rules, which can also be written up on a chart.

When children are presented with rules like this, they're usually interested in what's going to happen if they follow them or break them. Don't feel like you need to negotiate rewards or punishments with your child. Explain calmly that it's going to make you very happy as a parent to see them follow the rules, and that by following the rules, everyone will be able to get along better and avoid the arguments or fights that may have occurred in the past. Then explain the consequences that will be applied when the rules are disobeyed.

REGULATING FAMILY RULES

Address the process of effectively enforcing family rules. For example:

The way you enforce family rules is very similar to the way you would respond to the behaviours you want to encourage. The most important thing is to catch the child following the rules, use descriptive praise, and reward them with the same kinds of rewards you are using to encourage other behaviours (for example, physical affection, time with parent).

When a ground rule is broken, go through the same steps that you use for responding to misbehaviour. The only difference will be that if you are using particular consequences for different ground rules, you will implement the consequence instead of the time-out step.

Ask parents to recall the steps for responding to misbehaviour. Offer appropriate praise, and use Socratic questioning to guide the parents through the correction process.

Session 6: Midpoint Review of Strategies

Major Component

■ **MIDPOINT REVIEW OF CHILD-MANAGEMENT STRATEGIES**

Note: Due to the focus of this session, it may be omitted if the therapist is confident that parents are implementing the strategies as effectively as possible and the referred child is responding well.

REVIEW OF GOALS

This is the final session to focus exclusively on child behaviour and the respective child-management strategies. As such, it is important to address any outstanding issues regarding the implementation of these strategies, and to ensure the child is responding positively to them. The problem areas and respective goals identified in Session 4 form the basis of this review, each of which should be addressed in relation to the plan of action negotiated in the same session.

Beginning with the most significant problem area/goal:

1. Summarise the relevant issues and ask parents to comment on relevant changes that have occurred (both in their implementation and their child's behaviour).
2. If these outcomes do not indicate adequate progress, refer back to the corresponding plan of action to determine whether it has been enacted as agreed.
3. Renegotiate the plan of action for this problem area/goal by facilitating a problem-solving approach with parents, encouraging openness in the discussion of difficulties they may be facing.

HOMEWORK

Emphasise to parents the importance of focusing their efforts on the respective plan of action over the next week, explaining that the subsequent sessions will involve a shift in focus to broader parent/family issues that may be impacting on child behaviour.

Session
6

Sessions 7&8: Identifying and Planning Supports

Major Component

- **IDENTIFYING AND PLANNING SUPPORTS FOR PARENTS COPING WITH STRESS**

  Module 1: Time management

  Module 2: Anger management

  Module 3: Problem-solving skills

  Module 4: Pleasant events and social support

  Module 5: Cognitive coping skills

  Module 6: Partner-support training

SELECTION OF MODULES

This component involves a number of alternative modules that can be delivered in combination to meet the specific needs of families. The selection of modules is achieved using the client-centred process outlined below, in which the impact of systemic issues on the target child's behaviour is discussed and relevant goals are identified. At this stage, the therapist should have some knowledge of the issues and difficulties that may be compromising the wellbeing and functioning of parents. In the process of determining the modules most applicable to parents, existing knowledge should be used to guide parents in identifying the difficulties requiring attention.

Available modules are as follows, with indications specified for each:

MODULE NAME	INDICATIONS
(1) Time management	The parent is having difficulty organising or coordinating commitments, resulting in problems such as recurrent lateness for appointments or deadlines, or frequently uncompleted tasks.
(2) Anger management	The parent experiences frequent or disproportionate increases in anger, resulting in behaviours that are excessive or difficult to inhibit (for example, the parent often screams following minor disruptive acts, or frequently smacks a child despite disapproving of physical punishment).
(3) Problem-solving skills	The parent has difficulty deciding on the appropriate course of action for various problems, or is unable to condense complex problems into manageable tasks (for example, the client procrastinates, or impulsively applies the first apparent solution to a problem).

(4) Pleasant events and social support	For various reasons, the parent engages in few activities of personal interest, or limited social interactions (for example, the parent is too busy, unmotivated, or self-doubting to participate in enjoyable activities not directly related to their commitments as a parent). May be of particular relevance when symptoms of depression are apparent.
(5) Cognitive coping skills	The parent experiences symptoms of mild depression, or worries excessively about a range of potential problems (for example, the parent describes periods in which they feel down, uninterested, and lacking in motivation; the parent often feels overwhelmed or preoccupied with various issues or concerns).
(6) Partner-support training	This module addresses the importance and means of maintaining healthy relationships with partners and significant others. Due to the specificity of the problems addressed in this module and the amount of content included, particular care should be taken to establish that the module is warranted before progressing. The considerations relevant to this decision are addressed at the beginning of the module (that is, availability of partners, severity of relationship discord, problem perception, prior participation in skills training, and motivation and commitment).

STRUCTURING THE TWO SESSIONS

In structuring the parent self-care sessions, care should be taken to spread content as evenly as possible across the respective sessions. Begin each session with the standard procedure for welcoming clients and attending to events that have occurred over the previous week, and present an appropriate agenda for the session. Conclude the first session by setting appropriate homework, and review it at the commencement of the second session.

PARENT CARE

Explain how the parent self-care component fits into the conceptualisation of child behaviour presented at the commencement of the program. For example:

> You might remember that in one of our first sessions we spoke about the factors that can cause children to behave in different ways. One of those main factors was 'interactions between parents and children', which is what we have focused on in much of the work we've done together. Another important factor was 'things that affect us as parents'. This is an area that is sometimes neglected when people are doings things to improve their child's behaviour, but it can be really important.
>
> We are going to look at things that you can do to improve *your* own coping and wellbeing, and how doing that can bring about real improvements in your child's behaviour as well as *their* wellbeing.

Present a general rationale for addressing parent wellbeing:

> When you think about what's involved in parenting, there can be a trap where various aspects of parenting often result in feelings and reactions that make it harder to parent effectively. These are feelings like anger, agitation, and frustration. A lot of stuff that goes along with parenting and family life can be stressful, and these feelings are normal from time to time.

However, when we are feeling preoccupied with what's happening at work, or angry about the neighbours, or worried about finances, we have less attention to give to the immediate situation we are in with our children. It is also common for these feelings to interfere with our judgment about how best to respond to children in a given situation. It's obviously hard to feel in control when you are distracted by things that are on your mind.

Address the means by which parent stress can impact adversely on child behaviour:

There are also a couple of other ways that parent stress often impacts on children and their behaviour.

The *first way* is about setting an example for children. Often when we are feeling stressed, angry, frustrated, or agitated, we do things that we probably wouldn't want our children to do – maybe get irritable with others, or yell. Alternatively, when we use positive coping strategies, we can set a good example for children about the way to manage difficult feelings. So, the child can actually learn that when you feel upset by something, there are other ways to deal with it besides losing your temper.

The *second way* is sometimes less obvious. It's important to remember that when a child is around someone who feels unsettled, then they are going to also feel unsettled, and this can result in misbehaviour. You're probably aware yourself of what it's like when you spend time with someone who is feeling a particular way – maybe really anxious, or really down. You often notice yourself feeling the same way. So, this means that if we're feeling calm and relaxed when we are with our children, then they will be more likely to feel calm and relaxed too.

GOAL-SETTING AND SELECTION OF MODULES

Explain to parents that effective parenting is contingent upon a number of basic conditions:

There are a number of things that are required in order to parent effectively. For example, all parents need to be able to:

- manage competing demands with the time available
- feel in control of strong emotions such as anger
- feel confident dealing with everyday problems, rather than often feeling overwhelmed by them
- spend time and have friendships with other adults, and do things that are personally enjoyable
- be able to cope with feelings of worry, or a depressed mood
- (if in a relationship) be in a relationship that is supportive and enables you to parent as a team.

Invite parents to discuss their needs, in relation to the conditions presented above. For example:

Let's talk about what's important or relevant to you.

Facilitate this process by encouraging parents to consider the impact of various systemic issues on their own functioning, and on their parenting practices. If a range of issues are identified, help parents rank these according to the magnitude of this impact. Once these problem areas have been identified, it is important to set specific goals concerning the respective changes that need to occur. Finally, negotiate a course of action. Present parents with the general details of relevant modules, and invite them to comment on the options being presented.

MODULE 1: TIME MANAGEMENT

THE IMPORTANCE OF TIME MANAGEMENT TO PARENTS

Being in the role of parent involves not only a great number of competing demands, but a diversity of commitments that are found in few other roles. Parents are required to do a lot of things, and a lot of different things. One of the main sources of stress for parents can come from feeling overwhelmed by these commitments, and one of the most common laments you hear from parents is 'There is not enough time in the day'. Effective time management can create more time and therefore reduce stress.

By applying simple time-management principles you can use your energy doing the things you need to do, rather than expending it all just trying to work out how you are going to get around to everything. This means that as well as getting things done, time management can help you to do things in a more focused way with less distraction.

Time management is also particularly important for parents when it comes to organising time to do things for yourself and your own wellbeing.

EFFECTIVE TIME-MANAGEMENT PRACTICES

Time management involves working through a number of stages, making use of a number of basic strategies.

The What and When of Time Management

The initial task of time management is to determine what needs to be done in the relevant timeframe (for example, the upcoming week, month, and so on). Identifying clear and specific goals can facilitate this process. Both short- and long-term goals should be considered.

While it is hoped that all of these activities will be completed within this period, for various reasons it may not be possible to complete them all. The consequences of this eventuality can be limited by prioritising activities and attending to them in order of importance. This requires the consideration of all of the known activities requiring attention during the given period:

1. List all known commitments.
2. Rank these in terms of importance, considering the purpose of various commitments and the consequences of delaying them.

While prioritising involves decisions regarding the need to attend to some activities before others, a range of factors may limit the extent to which prioritised activities can be undertaken as planned. Factors that may dictate the times at which an activity can be completed include:

- the general context of the activity (for example, work, personal life, and so on)
- the duration of the activity
- financial means
- the availability of others involved in the activity
- whether or not activities need to be completed in a particular order.

The How of Time Management

Various strategies can be utilised in order to attend to commitments and tasks with greater efficiency. Apply these strategies creatively, experimenting to find out what works best for you:

- ***Keep a record of upcoming activities.*** Using a diary or calendar for this process can be useful, providing a tangible measure of time and allowing these commitments to be considered in relation to each other.
- ***Create a 'to do' list for each day.*** In addition to presenting prompts, such lists can provide motivation and a sense of achievement.
- ***Become aware of procrastination.*** Question why procrastination may be occurring, and remind yourself how you will feel when you complete the task.
- ***Utilise help from others.*** Accept help when it is offered, or ask for help, in exchange for reciprocal assistance at a later time.
- ***Develop reliable systems or methods for undertaking predictably difficult activities.*** This may involve working out a routine or a particular order that tasks involved in some process can be most efficiently performed. Such a process can be effective when experiencing recurrent problems with a task:
  1. Reflect on your most recent experience of attempting the task. Identify what went well as well as what problems occurred.
  2. Consider what you might be able to do differently next time to avoid these problems.
  3. When you are next faced with the respective task, attempt the proposed changes.
  4. Return to the first step and repeat the process until you arrive at the most satisfactory method for performing the task.

MODULE 2: ANGER MANAGEMENT

PRESENT THE RATIONALE FOR ANGER-MANAGEMENT TRAINING

Anger is part of the normal spectrum of emotions. There are many situations in which it may be a typical response; however, it can become a problem when it occurs too frequently or intensely, or leads to aggressive behaviour. When we understand it, however, anger can be controlled.

Because anger is a very acute emotion, many people are not aware that it involves a very subtle chain of events. The focus of anger management training involves understanding and recognising these events, and intervening at different points in the chain.

The process consists of:

A triggering event

↓

Our interpretation of the triggering event

↓

Physiological response

For example:

(Triggering event)

A boy walks across a clean floor with muddy feet

↓

(Interpretation of the triggering event)

The boy's mother thinks, 'Nobody appreciates the work I do to keep the house clean', and has a mental image of herself re-cleaning the floor, her back and legs aching.

↓

(Physiological response)

The mother's heart starts beating faster, her breathing becomes more rapid, and her muscles begin to feel tight.

PRESENT THE COMPONENTS OF ANGER MANAGEMENT

Recognising Triggers

When we understand what things are likely to trigger anger in us, it is easier for us to predict it. This can require careful consideration, because some events may only trigger anger when combined with some other factor or condition. For example, various circumstances can increase sensitivity to anger-triggering events (for example, tiredness, being in a crowded or noisy place, feeling hungry).

Cognitive Responses to Triggers

Become aware of the self-talk, or automatic thoughts, with which you respond to the events that typically trigger anger. When you are aware of the way you usually interpret or respond to such events, you can challenge these interpretations for accuracy, and replace them with thoughts that can help maintain self-control.

The first step is to evaluate these thoughts to determine how realistic they are. Such thoughts are often absolutistic (for example, 'I'll *always* have to put up with this', or 'This *never* happens to other people'). Alternatively, these thoughts are often catastrophic (for example, 'This is just going to get worse and worse', 'I'm going to lose my mind if this keeps up').

The aim is to replace these automatic thoughts with more realistic ones. Question the thoughts by identifying evidence for and against the interpretation or expectation.

In addition to challenging the rationality of automatic thoughts, such thoughts can be replaced with coping statements. These are thoughts that can apply to a wide range of situations. They can be effective in reminding the individual that they are in control. For example:

I've gotten through this before, and I can do it again.

Don't take it personally.

This is going to be difficult, but I can handle it.

Things are under control.

Recognising Physiological Responses

The physiological changes associated with anger can be addressed directly using relaxation techniques (for example, slow, deep breathing). However, as such responses escalate, this becomes increasingly difficult. It is therefore important to be able to recognise early physiological signs of anger so they can be addressed with minimal effort. The establishment of a regular relaxation routine can also decrease the likelihood of anger self-control difficulties.

Recognising Excessive Levels of Anger

Another important skill related to self-awareness is the ability to recognise when one's level of anger is so high that some kind of outburst is likely to soon occur. It is critical at such times to remove oneself from any environment in which people or belongings might be injured.

MODULE 3: PROBLEM-SOLVING SKILLS

While the problems facing parents are many and varied, it is possible to apply the same set of steps to solving problems in general:

STEP 1: DEFINE THE PROBLEM

When you become aware of a problem, the first step is to form a clear idea of the *outcome or goal* that you are aiming for, and the issues that represent *barriers* to that outcome.

Example:

> The problem for John's parents is that they have received a telephone call from his school principal, who has reported that John has been recently been getting into trouble for fighting with his peers.
>
> The desired outcome for such a situation is for John to stop fighting.
>
> There are a number of barriers to this outcome, things that make it hard for John's parents to reach this outcome. For example, they cannot personally supervise their son at the school, and they are not yet aware of the specific circumstances of the fighting.

STEP 2: BRAINSTORM SOLUTIONS

The next step is to think of what things might be done to overcome the identified barriers and reach the desired outcome. A number of potential solutions are generated using the *brainstorm* method. This means that ideas should be as creative and imaginative as possible, as they are not going to be evaluated at this point, but simply offered.

Example:

> (1) Ask John about his behaviour in a warm and supportive manner
>
> (2) Withdraw him from the school
>
> (3) Telephone the school to find out more details about John's behaviour
>
> (4) Send him to a psychiatrist
>
> (5) Hire a private investigator to monitor John's behaviour

STEP 3: NARROW DOWN THE POTENTIAL SOLUTIONS

Each potential solution will vary in relation to feasibility, and each will result in different consequences. These must be considered when attempting to select the most appropriate course of action. Begin by eliminating those that appear obviously unrealistic, narrowing down the options to those most feasible.

Example:

(1) Possible

(2) Based on what is known there is no reason to go so far

(3) Possible

(4) First need to find out if he is the one causing the trouble, or if he is being bullied, and so on

(5) Too expensive

STEP 4: SELECT THE MOST APPROPRIATE SOLUTION

Consider the advantages and disadvantages of the remaining options.

Example:

Option 1 pros	Option 1 cons
The problem is addressed without involving anyone outside the family	John might lie about his behaviour to avoid getting punished by his parents

STEP 5: CONSIDER HOW THE CHOSEN SOLUTION COULD BE IMPLEMENTED

Does it seem like a straightforward process, or are there other issues that must be first addressed? It may be the case that more than one of the generated solutions are chosen, and the order in which they are implemented may be relevant.

Example:

John's parents might decide to first implement option (1), and then follow this up with option (3).

MODULE 4: PLEASANT EVENTS AND SOCIAL SUPPORT

PRESENT A RATIONALE FOR INCREASING PLEASANT EVENTS AND SOCIAL SUPPORT

For many parents, the care of their child represents the main focus of their activities. For stay-at-home parents, as well as those in paid employment, it is common for home- and child-related activities to limit their participation in activities of personal or social interest. Limited exposure to pleasant events or social interaction can adversely affect the well-being of parents and their ability to cope with the ongoing demands of parenting. In order to raise a well-balanced child, parents need to have a well-balanced life, with satisfying personal interests and social relationships.

DISCUSS THE BENEFITS OF ACTIVITY

- Feelings of fatigue resulting from child-focused activities can often be overcome by engaging in activities of personal enjoyment.
- Participating in personal activities can distract us from various issues that may be stressful.
- Participation in personal or social activities involves planning, and can therefore provide the opportunity to experience the satisfaction of achieving goals. This can improve motivation in relation to more general commitments.
- Taking yourself out of your everyday setting and into a new environment with different people can help to provide a new perspective on various issues or problems.
- Many enjoyable and relaxing activities involve interaction with other people. This can lead to the development of new friendships and greater social support.
- The experience of a depressed mood is often coupled with a lack of motivation and feelings of general disinterest. While this makes it harder to get involved in activities that are not routine, forcing oneself to engage in an activity that has previously been enjoyable is one of the most reliable ways to lift one's mood.

DISCUSS THE PROCESS OF PLANNING ACTIVITIES

The process of participating in new activities involves a number of steps. There are also various guidelines that can be followed to get the most out of such activities.

When choosing activities, use a list such as that shown in the Pleasant Events Schedule. Consider both activities that have provided enjoyment in the past, perhaps before the children were born, as well as previously unattempted activities that appeal.

Include a mix of activities that can be enjoyed with minimal preparation and those requiring more planning. Rank these in order of how easy they will be to undertake.

While it is good to engage in these activities spontaneously when other commitments allow, for activities requiring preparation it is important to set aside time to participate in the activity. This may involve marking dates on calendars or in diaries. The most important step is to stick to these dates.

Attend to any other issues associated with the activity. This may involve arranging for child-minding, making bookings, obtaining particular materials, and so on.

One useful strategy for encouraging yourself to follow through with a planned event is to invite another person. People are less likely to cancel if it means having to explain why to someone else.

Enter the activity with an open mind. Maintain an attitude of experimentation, finding out what kind of things are enjoyable and satisfying. This can be useful for avoiding disappointment following an event. Remember that some activities will be more enjoyable than others, and that some people are more pleasant to be with than others.

(Provide parents with a pleasant events schedule form in addition to handouts.)

MODULE 5: COGNITIVE COPING SKILLS

This component does not represent an intervention for clinical depression, but rather, psychoeducation addressing coping skills that can be applied to manage an intermittently depressed mood or feelings of being overwhelmed.

INTRODUCE THE COMPONENT

Feelings of sadness are normal and may be related to any number of experiences related to parenting or personal life. However, when the duration or intensity of such feelings interferes with family relationships or responsibilities, it is important to know what can be done to overcome them.

INTRODUCE THE COGNITIVE MODEL

Ask the client to recall a specific time in the last few days when they noticed a negative change in their mood.

Invite the client to describe the situation they were in at the time.

Ask the client what they were thinking at the time.

Using the client's own words, repeat the automatic thoughts stated.

Clarify the emotional response associated with these thoughts, either by reflecting feelings reported earlier, or by asking the client to share these.

In the context of the cognitive model, discuss the material disclosed. Present the model diagrammatically, making explicit the relationship between the three components (situation → thought → emotion).

When outlining the model, include the following key points:

- All emotions are preceded by some thought or belief or interpretation.
- The 'situation' may be a very specific or subtle aspect of some set of circumstances, or an internal event such as a physiological sensation or a memory or thought.
- Thoughts are not always conscious; however, they can be accessed by asking yourself various questions.

Invite the client to comment on the respective conceptualisation.

ADDRESS THE ROLE AND NATURE OF COGNITIVE DISTORTIONS

Introduce the discussion of the following concepts, explaining that there are a number of basic distinctions made when applying the respective model to cognitive processes. For example:

> In a moment we are going to talk about the strategies that are used to gain control over these thoughts, but first it is important that you understand the basic distinctions that we make between different thought processes. This terminology might seem a little confusing at first, but understanding these distinctions is really important before we go any further.

Describe the relevant concepts, including the following key points:

Automatic Thoughts

- The term 'automatic thoughts' is used to describe all the spontaneous thoughts that run through our minds.
- These include both positive and negative thoughts that can be in the form of both verbal statements and images.
- These thoughts can be conscious and explicit, or unconscious and accessible only through self-questioning.
- Automatic thoughts may or may not make sense or be accurate or realistic.
- It is the negative automatic thoughts that are associated with a negative mood.

Refer to examples of negative automatic thoughts suggested by the client's dialogue.

Core Beliefs

- Core beliefs (or schemes) are fundamental beliefs that an individual holds about themselves and more general aspects of life.
- Like automatic thoughts, core beliefs can be positive or negative. Examples of negative core beliefs are 'The world is unfair', and 'I am worthless'.
- These beliefs are the outcome of our life experiences and therefore reflect the influences of family, culture, interpersonal relationships, and personal experiences.
- They influence the automatic thoughts with which an individual will respond to a given situation and can therefore function as biases towards particular ways of interpreting or responding to the events in our lives.
- Core beliefs can also be activated by significant events or crises. When activated, a core belief becomes more powerful in shaping the thoughts of the individual and, in turn, their mood.

Logical Errors

Explain that the negative automatic thoughts of people who suffer from depressed moods often contain errors that create a negative bias.

Give the client the Evaluating Automatic Thoughts handout, commenting on the nature and purpose of the content.

Invite the client to look through the list and find those that might be present in their thinking.

INSTRUCT THE CLIENT IN THE IDENTIFICATION OF AUTOMATIC THOUGHTS

Ask the client to think of a time during the week when they felt upset.

Ask the client what was going through their mind at the time.

Present the client with the following strategies and guidelines for identifying automatic thoughts:

1. When identifying automatic thoughts, express them as statements such as 'My child is going to end up is prison', rather than questions such as 'I wonder if my child will end up in prison'.
2. Attend to thoughts that correspond with a change or increase in emotion. These thoughts, or the changes in emotion they produce, may be distracting and interfere with the ability to concentrate on some task.
3. During an event, ask yourself questions such as:
   - What just went through my mind?
   - If I had to take a guess, what would I guess I was thinking about?
   - Am I picturing something in my mind?
4. When trying to access thoughts from a situation after it occurs, try to imagine yourself in that situation, describing the scenario in as much detail as possible, or imagining it as vividly as possible.
5. Define vague or ambiguous concepts (for example, What exactly do I mean by 'disaster'?).

INSTRUCT THE CLIENT IN THE PROCESS OF CHALLENGING NEGATIVE AUTOMATIC THOUGHTS

Introduce the component, stating the aim of challenging automatic thoughts. For example:

> The aim of challenging automatic thoughts is to replace the unrealistic assumptions or beliefs responsible for a negative mood with more realistic and hopeful alternatives.

Present parents with al thoughts record form, which is used to identify and challenge automatic thoughts, and discuss the steps in this process.

Present and discuss the questions that can be used to challenge the validity of automatic thoughts and generate alternative, adaptive responses:

1. What is the evidence?
   What is the evidence that supports this idea?
   What is the evidence against this idea?
2. Is there an alternative explanation?
3. What is the worst that could happen? Could I live through it?
   What is the best that could happen?
   What is the most realistic outcome?
4. What is the effect of my believing the automatic thought?
   What could be the effect of changing my thinking?
5. What should I do about it?
6. What would I tell ________ (a friend) if they were in the same situation?

Discuss the Differences Between Challenging Thoughts as They Occur and Retrospectively

The process of challenging negative automatic thoughts is quite different depending on where and when it is being undertaken.

Retrospective consideration of a mood change:

- Use the thoughts record form, recording the situation, automatic thoughts, emotions, adaptive responses, and emotional outcome.
- Plan to put yourself in situations that allow you to collect evidence in support of your new adaptive response.

At the time of a mood change:

- Take a moment to stop and identify automatic thoughts.
- Consider whether the current thoughts are similar to any that you have challenged previously, and make use of any previously successful responses.

Present Additional Strategies for Overcoming a Negative Mood

- *Utilising coping statements.* Take note of adaptive responses that can be applied to numerous negative thoughts. These can function as coping statements that may be useful while in the midst of a stressful situation in which there are limited opportunities to give attention to the specific automatic thoughts currently occurring.
- *Maintaining a 'positives diary'.* Keeping a positives diary involves recording positive events and experiences that disconfirm typical negative automatic thoughts. The aim of it is to compensate for the negative bias in automatic thoughts by shifting the balance in favour of thoughts that will enhance your self-esteem and increase motivation. For example, if you became aware of recurrent negative automatic thoughts related to your abilities as a parent (for example, 'I never do anything good for my child', or 'If my child misbehaves in public I won't know what to do'), your positives diary might include entries such as:

  > *Today I woke up early and took Aaron to the park. We both had a great time ...*

  and

  > *Today I went shopping with Aaron and he threw a tantrum when I wouldn't buy him a toy. I calmly explained my decision to him and followed through with it. He calmed down quite soon afterwards, and I realised that I am pretty prepared for situations like that.*

MODULE 6: PARTNER-SUPPORT TRAINING

ASSESSMENT CONSIDERATIONS

Partner-support training (PST) will not be appropriate for all families presenting with child-conduct problems. An assessment of the caregiving environment is therefore essential, and the following factors should be considered:

Availability of Partners

Partner-support training requires the participation of two caregivers who have frequent and regular contact with each other and the referred child. It may be appropriate when relationship communication problems are precipitating, or being precipitated by, child-behaviour problems. This may be indicated by parental disagreement over issues such as methods of discipline, a depressed mood in one or both parents, or temper outbursts that serve as a model to the child.

Severity of Relationship Discord

Severe relationship discord will require intensive therapy, beyond the scope of short-term partner-support training. Alternatively, some families may exhibit adequate levels of communicative, supportive, and problem-solving skills prior to intervention. In such cases, either partner-support training may not be warranted or it may need to be adapted to the needs of the target family.

Problem Perception

It can be difficult to solicit the active participation of partners in child-management training when they differ in perceptions of the nature and causes of the child's problem behaviour. This difficulty is often observed with fathers. For example, a father might believe that the child's mother is to blame because the child rarely misbehaves in his presence.

Prior Participation in Skills Training

Gains from partner-support training are predicated on a familiarity with the procedures presented during child-management training. Partner-support training should therefore be scheduled only for caregivers who have actively participated in prior components of the program.

Motivation and Commitment

The commitment of caregivers to partner-support training can be compromised by an insufficient understanding of why the respective component is being undertaken, and what it involves. All caregivers should therefore be fully informed of the nature and aims of the training procedures, and their consent should be obtained.

THE STRUCTURE OF PARTNER-SUPPORT TRAINING

The activities involved in partner-support training are undertaken in four components:

1. When a problem is occurring
2. Casual discussions
3. Problem-solving discussions
4. Giving and receiving feedback.

WHEN A PROBLEM IS OCCURRING

Introduce the component and present a rationale emphasising the importance of maintaining a cohesive partnership while parenting. For example:

> With most of the work we have done so far, the focus has been on the way you respond to your child's behaviour. Most of the situations we have discussed have been ones in which the child does something, and the parent who happens to be nearby interacts with them in a particular way. However, it's important to realise that when two parents or caregivers are present, the way that both parents interact with each other in the process of parenting can really mean the difference between success and failure with these strategies.
>
> The most important thing is to be able to support each other's parenting behaviour and present a united front when dealing with a child's behaviour. However, this is often difficult. We're going to talk about some common problems that occur, and then look at some practical strategies for working together as a team.

ISSUE 1: Disagreement Over Household Rules

Comment on the possible reasons for this problem, explaining how it can impact on child behaviour, and provide an example scenario. For example:

> It is common for parents to have different expectations regarding the way children should behave. If you were to talk about the rules about behaviour that your own parents had when you were growing up, you would probably notice that there were different things that you were each allowed to get away with, and different things you were punished for.
>
> However, different expectations about child behaviour can become a problem when parents enforce different rules with the same children. For example, if a father likes the children to take the initiative to do housework or cooking without being asked, while the mother wants the children to wait until they are asked so they can be supervised, it would be easy to understand the children getting into trouble for breaking the mother's rule. These kinds of mixed messages can be even more confusing to a child when parents argue about the rule in front of the child.

Sessions 7&8

Clarify the ideas illustrated in the example. For example:

> In this example the child probably wouldn't respect the rule because his father doesn't. His mother's rule has been undermined by a parental disagreement. Children need to know the *where, what, and how* of behavioural rules. Children rely on their parents for these guidelines. It is therefore important to work together to agree on a set of household rules that you are both satisfied with.

ISSUE 2: Disagreement Over Discipline

Discuss the potential impact of discipline disagreement on child behaviour, explaining how it can exacerbate misbehaviour rather than reduce it. For example:

> Disagreement over the methods used to manage misbehaviour can also be confusing to children and result in increased misbehaviour. If punishment is inconsistent or varies in intensity it will not decrease the misbehaviour. On the contrary, it may often make the child behaviour even worse because the child

feels that the punishment is unfair (for example, 'Last time nothing happened to me!'). If a child knows that punishment consistently follows misbehaviour, the behaviour is likely to decrease and the child will not feel hurt or discouraged by the punishment.

ISSUE 3: Fighting in Front of Children

Discuss the potential impact of overt parental conflict in the presence of children, explaining the process of modelling. For example:

> While couples may fight from time to time, this is most likely to impact on children if it is happening in front of them. This is because children imitate their parents. If a child sees or hears yelling, requests being disregarded, or people being ignored, they will soon do the same. However, we can take advantage of this need to imitate by behaving with our partners the way we would like our children to behave with us and other people. If your children see you remaining calm, listening to others, and doing your best to help or comply with others, then they will do the same.

ISSUE 4: Not Sharing Workloads

Discuss the importance of cooperating in high-risk situations. For example:

Sessions 7&8

> There are many situations encountered regularly by parents that require more attention, hands, or eyes than one person is able to provide. During meal preparation, housework, and mealtimes, your attention is divided among different tasks and it is hard to supervise your children. It is no coincidence then that these are also the situations in which child behaviour is most likely to be a problem. However, difficulties with child behaviour can be decreased dramatically in such situations if the workload is divided between two parents with, for example, one parent minding the children while the other is occupied.

ISSUE 5: Being Tough Versus Being Soft

Ask parents to consider the following situation:

> It's time for dinner, and Aaron's mother asks him to put his game away. He's saying, 'I want to keep playing'. (In mother's role) 'Come on, tea is ready'. (Child's role) 'Oh, I'll just be a minute'. (Mother's role) 'Come on Aaron, I said to put them away now'. Aaron ignores his mother and keeps playing. Then his father says, 'You heard your mother. Now put those away immediately'. So, Aaron says 'Okay' and complies.

Ask the parents what happened in this scenario, guiding them to recognise that the child's mother was the 'soft one', and his father the 'tough one'.

Then, clarify the process that is likely to be observed in such a family. For example:

> From observing a situation like this, it's likely that people in the family are in the habit of doing certain things and expecting certain things.
>
> Aaron has got into the habit of waiting for his father to intervene before he complies with his mother's instructions. The mother does not back up her instructions because she is in the habit of waiting for her husband to intervene. The father is used to intervening to ensure that Aaron does what his mother says.

Ask the parents what is likely to happen when Aaron's father is not present, or otherwise occupied, guiding them to recognise that Aaron will be unwilling to comply with requests despite his mother's repeated instructions.

Explain how such traps can be avoided by parents responding to child behaviour with mutual consistency. For example:

> To avoid this kind of trap, it is very important that *both* parents follow through with their own instructions to the child. It's good to back each other up as parents, but getting into the habit of relying on your partner to always discipline the children (or never discipline the children) is not good for either parent's relationship with the child.
>
> We don't want the child to see one tough parent and one softy. We want the child to see two fair parents who expect to be listened to, and so on.

How to Act When a Child Misbehaves in the Presence of Both Parents

Present the following guidelines and strategies for responding to child misbehaviour when both parents are present, clarifying each as appropriate:

1. Remain calm.

   For example, use a calm voice when speaking to both the child and your partner.
2. Try not to interfere if your partner is dealing with the child.

   That is, do not 'come to the rescue' by being the tough partner. The parent who gave the instructions to the child should follow them through.
3. Help your partner if you can see they need it.

   For example, if your spouse is looking after one child and the other children start to misbehave, you could help by tending to the other children.
4. Back each other up by not giving contradictory instructions to the child.

   This is something that can require a bit of advance planning. So, take notice of situations in which you and your partner have different expectations of child behaviour, and come to a mutually satisfactory compromise.
5. Ensure that feedback you have for your partner is presented in a non-confrontational way and provides constructive input.

   To do this, never comment on each other's behaviour until the problem is over and you are more relaxed. Also, try not to blame or criticise each other.
6. After the problem is over, discuss it together and, if necessary, arrange a problem-solving discussion.

CASUAL DISCUSSIONS

Introduce the component and present a rationale emphasising the importance of establishing effective communication habits and increasing consistency of child-management techniques between parents. For example:

> You're probably aware that many of the problems that occur with couples are related to communication difficulties. Good communication practices can be important in any adult relationship, but when the couple are relying on each other to do something as involved as raising a child, effective communication becomes absolutely critical.

Introduce the idea of holding casual discussions, explaining the basic rationale and activities involved. For example:

> One way of maintaining good communication is by putting aside a little time each day to talk to each other about the children and any other family matters. We use the term 'casual discussions' to refer to discussions that are not deliberately organised, but occur regularly at times when one or both partners would like to share information.
>
> We are going to look at a specific way of structuring discussions that maximises mutual understanding about your attitudes and behaviours as parents, and helps you to encourage and support each other in your child-management efforts.

Describe the common problems that can prevent the effective use of such discussions, and discuss each in appropriate detail. For example:

> While most parents attempt to discuss general family matters on a regular basis, these discussions can often be ineffective due to a number of things.

ISSUE 1: No Actual Discussion Takes Place

This can occur in a number of common scenarios. For example, a home-duties parent may try to report the events of the day to a working partner as soon as they step through the door. Alternatively, a working parent may try to engage a home-duties partner in a discussion requiring concerted thought when the partner has their first opportunity to relax after running around after the children.

Whatever the reason may be, when parents stop talking regularly family rifts begin, and it is likely that:

- parents will not present a united front to their children
- parents will not be consistent in their child-management techniques
- family problems will grow rather than disappear
- children will consistently misbehave.

ISSUE 2: Discussions Do Not Change Anything

A second common problem occurs when parents frequently discuss child-related issues and difficulties yet nothing eventuates from these discussions and things do not improve.

There are three common explanations for this:

1. During the discussion problems are identified, but no solution is reached, and no plans are made.
2. Parents disagree about what the problem is, or even disagree that there is a problem.
3. One parent may feel that the problem only occurs with the other parent. As such, they do not listen to the discussion; they are not interested.

ISSUE 3: Discussions Are Unpleasant

Like any other activity, if discussions are unpleasant people will do their best to avoid them. Unfortunately, such avoidance can occur at the times at which discussions may be most useful, such as following family outings. The main reasons that discussions are aversive include nagging, ignoring, ridicule, and sarcasm.

However, if these discussions are conducted in a certain way, they can become an important way of supporting and encouraging each other.

Address the importance of timing. For example:

> First, it's important to make sure that you speak to each other every day, at a time that is convenient for both partners; for example, when you get home from work, after an outing, or during dinner. However, the important thing is to make an agreement about such times rather than assuming that the chosen time is convenient for the other partner.

Address the process of conducting discussions. For example:

> Second, try to follow the steps for conducting casual discussions that are listed on your handout. You will note that this routine encourages you to *listen* to each other, to provide *feedback* on each other's behaviour, to ask *questions* of each other, and to schedule a *problem-solving session* if necessary. Don't try to solve any problems during these discussions. Just take time to listen to each other. If something good happened, praise it and enjoy your partner's success. If something unpleasant happened, get the details and offer to help.

Steps for conducting casual discussions

- Ask your partner about their day.
- Show you are listening and interested.
- Ask how the children have been in your absence.

If no problem occurred: ↓	If a problem occurred: ↓
Ask what the children have been doing and give positive feedback to your partner.	Ask for a clear description of what happened. Listen carefully and show that you are listening and interested.

- Ask how your partner dealt with the situation.
- Again, show you are listening and interested.

If the problem was handled in a way consistent with the program: ↓	If your partner had trouble handling the problem: ↓
Give positive feedback to your partner.	1. Give positive feedback on any successful aspects of how they handled the problem. 2. Make a time to sit down together and have a problem-solving discussion.

- Finally, offer to do something to help avoid the problem next time (for example, looking after your son while your wife bathes your daughter).

PROBLEM-SOLVING DISCUSSIONS

Introduce the component and present a rationale emphasising the importance of applying a logical structure to discussions focused on the solution of complicated problems. For example:

> **As parents, you cannot avoid all problems, but you can prevent them from developing into severe problems, and you can overcome many as well.**

To do this, you both need to work together as a united front, as a team who coordinates your behaviour to achieve mutually agreeable goals. This requires a number of skills and routines that should become habits for both of you.

Address the common difficulties encountered when attempting problem-solving discussions, discussing each in appropriate detail.

ISSUE 1: Disagreement Over the Problem

What is a problem to one person may not be a problem to another. In order to solve a problem, the most fundamental requirement is that both partners agree on what it is.

There are no easy solutions to this issue, but the first step is to sit down and talk about it. This means saying how you feel about the situation and listening to the other's point of view. The goals should be to reach a mutually agreeable definition of what is acceptable to both partners, and what is not. At times, a compromise may be the only solution.

ISSUE 2: Disagreement Over the Solution

After agreeing on what needs to change, the next step is to identify potential solutions. Disagreement can be a common difficulty at this step. One parent might believe that waiting is the most appropriate way to handle the problem, while the other might feel that it needs to be addressed immediately.

A useful approach at this stage is to write down *all possible solutions*, and then discuss them one at a time before making any decisions. Weigh up the pros and cons of each potential solution, having your say and listening to your partner's view. The process of agreeing on the most appropriate solution may involve compromise and, when possible, the most effective way of identifying the best solution is to put it into practice and observe the outcome.

ISSUE 3: Disagreement Over the Implementation of the Solution

The next step is to translate the agreed upon course of action into a practical plan so that each of you knows exactly what to do when the problem occurs.

Implementing a course of action in a consistent way is particularly important, as a failure to do so can prevent you from finding out how useful the agreed upon solution actually is.

Provide each other with plenty of encouragement and motivation, and keep an open mind. If the intended course of action falls short of the goal, do not get discouraged. Arrange another problem-solving discussion and try again. Sooner or later you will find the solution that works.

ISSUE 4: Difficulties Finding the Time and the Place

To be conducted effectively, problem-solving discussions require a high degree of concentration and cooperation. You cannot achieve this unless you are comfortable and relaxed and can work uninterrupted. As such, it is essential that you and your partner can negotiate a mutually convenient time when you can be alone and will not be interrupted by children or other commitments.

This might mean waiting until the children are in bed and you can spread out any paperwork over a table.

Guidelines for Conducting Problem-Solving Discussions

Present and discuss the respective guidelines:

Agree upon a mutual time and place to talk to each other about any problems you are currently experiencing. It should be when you are both calm and will not be interrupted by the children.

Identify the problem behaviour as specifically as possible. Try to deal with one problem at a time. Write down the problem as clearly as possible. Check that you both agree on what needs to change.

Brainstorm together, thinking of as many possible solutions as you can, and write these down clearly.

Discuss each solution, weighing its pros and cons, its likelihood of success, whether it is practical to use, and any problems that might arise.

Choose the best solution(s) by mutual agreement or compromise.

Plan a strategy for using the solution. Be specific in working out exactly what you will both say and do when the problem occurs.

Plan to **review** how the solution is going by arranging another meeting together.

Sessions 7&8

GIVING AND RECEIVING FEEDBACK

Guidelines for Giving Constructive Feedback

Introduce the component, providing a brief rationale and emphasising the importance of each partner being able to effectively speak and listen. Also emphasise the idea that such skills can be attained by following a number of basic guidelines. For example:

> Giving effective feedback to each other involves communicating opinions in a way that makes your partner feel good about your ideas, and helps them change their behaviour for the better. These aims can only be achieved by knowing how to speak and listen effectively. However, these skills can be learnt by following a number of basic guidelines.
>
> So, we're going to look at the things you should be doing whenever you comment on your partner's behaviour.

1. ***Start with the positives.*** When offering feedback, it helps the receiver to first hear what you liked about their behaviour. If the positive is heard first, the negative is more likely to be listened to, and acted upon. For example:

   > 'I felt you did the right thing by putting John into time-out when he was screaming. I did feel you were a bit rough with him when you pushed him into the room, however.'

2. ***Be specific.*** Try to avoid general or vague comments. Statement such as 'You were brilliant' or 'Try harder next time' do not give any details and are therefore of limited use in helping the person change. Try to pinpoint exactly what the person did rather than using general labels or suggestions. For example:

'You spoke in a very pleasant voice when he was misbehaving today.'

or

'I feel that you kept arguing with John when you could have acted and used back-up such as time-out.'

3. *Offer alternatives.* Suggest at least one thing that the person could have done differently. In doing so, turn the negative into a positive suggestion. For example:

   'I felt that instead of ignoring Judy's swearing, you could have told her you didn't like it, and backed up your instruction.'

4. *Describe, do not judge.* Describe what happened, not your judgment of whether it was 'good', 'bad', 'nasty', 'nice', and so forth. For example:

   'You are using child-directed play techniques really well when you play with the children and it really seems to be helping them to play cooperatively.'

   is better than

   'You play well with the children.'

5. *Own the feedback.* It is easy to say to the other person 'you are ...', as if you are offering a universally agreed-upon opinion. Remember that when you are giving feedback it is your opinion, and thus it is better to start with openings like:

   'I feel that ...'

   'In my opinion ...'

Guidelines for Receiving Feedback

Introduce the component, making reference to the importance of receiving feedback effectively if we are to achieve positive changes in our behaviour. For example:

> While we may think of ourselves as being in a passive role when it's our turn to receive feedback, it's important that we know how to make the most out of the feedback provided, and to remember that the purpose of feedback is to improve the way we do things.
>
> So, we're going to look now at things you can do to get the most out of feedback from your partner. These guidelines can also be used in other settings.

1. *Listen to the feedback rather than immediately rejecting or arguing with it.* While it can be uncomfortable to hear, it can result in positive outcomes. Remember that people do have their opinions about you. They will have their own perceptions of your behaviour, and it can help to be aware of these.
2. *Be clear about what is being said.* Try to avoid jumping to conclusions or becoming immediately defensive, otherwise people may limit their feedback or you may not be able to make full use of it. Make sure you understand the feedback before you respond to it. A useful technique can be to paraphrase or repeat the feedback, to check that you have understood.
3. *Ask for the feedback you want but do not get.* If feedback pertaining to important activities is not provided, it is important to elicit it. The feedback initially provided may

be restricted to one aspect of our behaviour and we may have to request specific feedback that is not volunteered.

4. ***Decide what you will do as a result of the feedback.*** Remember that the aim of receiving feedback is to help us change our behaviour for the better. So when feedback is available, consider how you might behave next time the situation occurs. In this way, the feedback will not be wasted.

HOMEWORK

- Experiment with casual discussions.
- Conduct a problem-solving discussion regarding an issue of current relevance that each partner feels comfortable experimenting with.
- Take turns presenting each other with feedback pertaining to some chosen event.

Session 9: Review and Relapse Prevention

Major Component

■ **OVERALL REVIEW AND RELAPSE PREVENTION**

This is the final session of the program, so it is important to ensure that the parents feel capable of continuing to implement the strategies learnt after therapy has ended. Highlight that problem behaviours may occur in the future, but also emphasise that the parents now possess the skills needed to effectively manage them. This can be demonstrated by discussing hypothetical future scenarios and how the parents would approach them. A final review of progress and all of the strategies presented during the program is also important in the final session, as it helps to identify any last areas that you may need to discuss and to tie everything together for the parents.

REVIEW PROGRESS

Invite the parents to comment on any promising aspects of the child's response to treatment, followed by less successful aspects. Encourage parents to suggest explanations for areas of limited success. If parents have neglected any relevant goals/problem areas addressed earlier in treatment, refer to these and assess progress in relation to each of these.

Invite parents to suggest issues that may be directly or indirectly limiting this progress. If the therapist is aware of relevant issues not presented, address these with the parents. Collaboratively identify long-term goals for the parents relating to issues such as strategies that may require further development, or particular settings that remain problematic. This discussion should also acknowledge the systemic issues addressed in the previous sessions.

It may be useful to return to the specific treatment components to which they pertain, providing more detailed attention to relevant procedural or conceptual issues. Utilise role-play methods wherever appropriate. Alternatively, if these issues are beyond the scope of any treatment component, encourage the parents to employ a problem-solving approach.

REVIEW OF TREATMENT COMPONENTS

Refer sequentially to the strategies presented over the course of treatment, commenting on the basic rationale for each. Emphasise the clients' strengths in their correct application of these strategies, and encourage clients to think of additional situations in which they could use such approaches.

RELAPSE PREVENTION

The process of concluding treatment should be discussed openly, with the therapist inviting parents to share any concerns or feelings regarding their independent implementation of the respective strategies in the future. Discuss the possibility that problem behaviours may return or change in nature or severity over time, while emphasising the idea that the parents now possess the tools necessary to combat a broad range of potential problems.

CHALLENGE PARENTS WITH HYPOTHETICAL SCENARIOS

Present a series of hypothetical behaviour problems, challenging parents to generate appropriate actions based on the strategies they have learnt throughout the program.

Use Socratic questioning throughout this process, directing parents when necessary towards the correct use of the relevant strategies while allowing them sufficient independence to demonstrate their capability. If parents suggest a tendency towards punishment methods alone as the first means of dealing with behaviour problems, remind them of the principle of 'positives before negatives' when deciding on behaviour-change strategies.

SECTION 3:
Handouts

Handouts for Session 3:

Possible Causes of Child Behaviour

Responding to Good Behaviour

Stop Misbehaviour

Possible Causes of Child Behaviour

GENETICS AND BIOLOGY

- The child's temperament
- The child's health
- Developmental disabilities

PARENT–CHILD INTERACTIONS

- Accidental rewards for misbehaviour
- Learning through watching
- Ignoring desirable behaviour
- How instructions are given
- Ineffective punishment

THINGS AFFECTING PARENTS

- Parents' levels of stress
- Marital conflict
- Lack of social support
- Financial stress

Responding to Good Behaviour

Watch out for the following behaviours:

1. ______________________________

2. ______________________________

3. ______________________________

4. ______________________________

5. ______________________________

When you see them, use the following rewards:

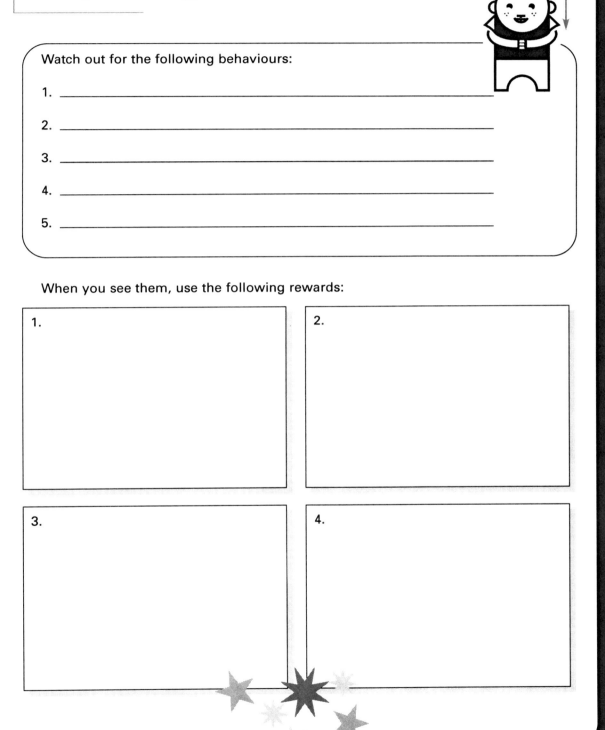

1.	2.
3.	4.

Stop Misbehaviour

This sequence boosts parent control and ends misbehaviour before it becomes a battle. The more it is used, the more children LISTEN!

EVERY TIME YOUR CHILD MISBEHAVES:

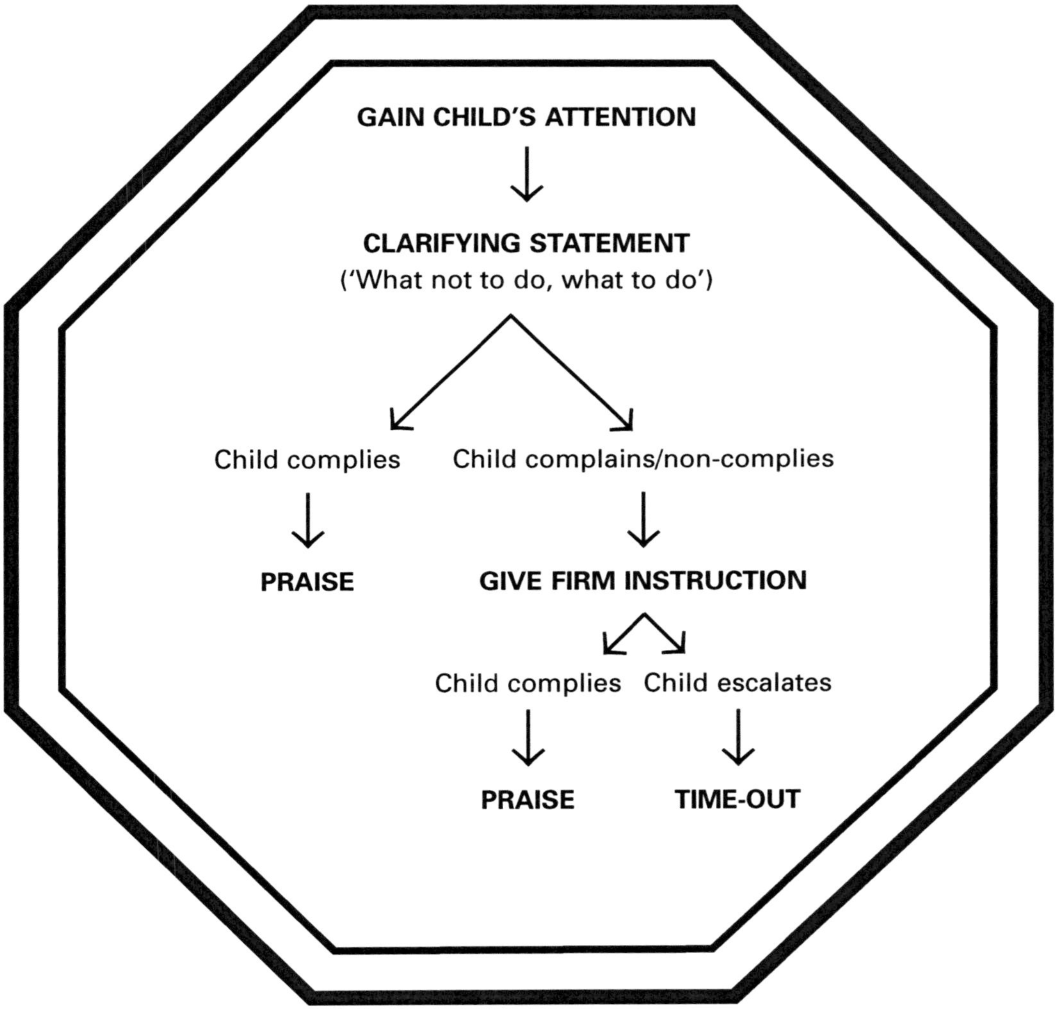

Handouts for Session 5:

Managing Sibling Conflict

Boredom-Busters

Managing Sibling Conflict

FOSTER POSITIVE PLAY

- Reward cooperative play and sharing.
- Reward periods of non-fighting.
- Make sure both children are rewarded as a team.
- Spend time with each child individually and as a pair.
- Reward children for coming and telling you about nice, shared activities.

DEAL EFFECTIVELY WITH ARGUMENTS

- Try not to listen to tell-taling (use planned ignoring).
- Minimise refereeing. If arguing needs to be stopped, apply blame equally across the children. There is little point trying to figure out who started it.
- Punish each child equally and briefly by either separating the children for a brief period or removing the object of the argument for a short period (for example, TV, a toy).
- If arguing persists, separate the children by specifying activities and locations that are apart.

Boredom-Busters

BEFORE ENTERING THE SITUATION

- Discuss appropriate and inappropriate behaviours with the child.
- Check that the child is aware of the rules relevant to the setting.
- Decide on, and organise, a number of appropriate engaging activities.

IN THE SITUATION

- Praise appropriate child behaviours.
- Provide a different activity before they lose interest in a current activity.
- Be creative and resourceful.

FOLLOWING THE SITUATION

- Give the child feedback about what they did well in the situation.
- Set goals for the next time.

Handouts for Sessions 7 & 8:

Module 1: Time Management

Module 2: Anger Management

Module 3: Problem-Solving Skills

Module 4: Pleasant Events and Social Support

Module 5: Cognitive Coping Skills

Module 6: Partner-Support Training

Module 1: Time Management

PARENTS AND TIME MANAGEMENT

Being in the role of parent involves not only a great number of competing demands, but a diversity of commitments that are found in few other roles. Parents are required to do a lot of things, and a lot of different things. One of the main sources of stress for parents can come from feeling overwhelmed by these commitments, and one of the most common laments you hear from parents is 'There is not enough time in the day'. Effective time management can create more time and therefore reduce stress.

By applying simple time-management principles you can use your energy doing the things you need to do, rather than expending it all just trying to work out how you are going to get around to everything. This means that as well as getting things done, time management can help you to do things in a more focused way with less distraction.

Time management is also particularly important for parents when it comes to organising time to do things for yourself and your own wellbeing.

EFFECTIVE TIME-MANAGEMENT PRACTICES

Time management involves working through a number of stages, making use of a number of basic strategies.

→ The What and When of Time Management

The initial task of time management is to determine what needs to be done in the relevant timeframe (for example, the upcoming week, month, and so on). Identifying clear and specific goals can facilitate this process. Both short- and long-term goals should be considered.

While it is hoped that all of these activities will be completed within this period, for various reasons it may not be possible to complete them all. The consequences of this eventuality can be limited by prioritising activities and attending to them in order of importance. This requires the consideration of all of the known activities requiring attention during the given period:

- ✔ List all known commitments.
- ✔ Rank these in terms of importance, considering the purpose of various commitments and the consequences of delaying them.

While prioritising involves decisions regarding the need to attend to some activities before others, a range of factors may limit the extent to which prioritised activities can be undertaken as planned. Factors that may dictate the times at which an activity can be completed include:

- ✔ the general context of the activity (for example, work, personal life, and so on)
- ✔ the duration of the activity
- ✔ financial means
- ✔ the availability of others involved in the activity
- ✔ whether or not activities need to be completed in a particular order.

→ The How of Time Management

Various strategies can be utilised in order to attend to commitments and tasks with greater efficiency. Apply these strategies creatively, experimenting to find out what works best for you:

- ✔ ***Keep a record of upcoming activities.*** Using a diary or calendar for this process can be useful, providing a tangible measure of time and allowing these commitments to be considered in relation to each other.
- ✔ ***Create a 'to do' list for each day.*** In addition to presenting prompts, such lists can provide motivation and a sense of achievement.
- ✔ ***Become aware of procrastination.*** Question why procrastination may be occurring, and remind yourself how you will feel when you complete the task.
- ✔ ***Utilise help from others.*** Accept help when it is offered, or ask for help, in exchange for reciprocal assistance at a later time.
- ✔ ***Develop reliable systems or methods for undertaking predictably difficult activities.*** This may involve working out a routine or a particular order that tasks involved in some process can be most efficiently performed. Such a process can be effective when experiencing recurrent problems with a task:

    1. Reflect on your most recent experience of attempting the task. Identify what went well as well as what problems occurred.
    2. Consider what you might be able to do differently next time to avoid these problems.
    3. When you are next faced with the respective task, attempt the proposed changes.
    4. Return to the first step and repeat the process until you arrive at the most satisfactory method for performing the task.

Module 2: Anger Management

Anger is part of the normal spectrum of emotions. There are many situations in which it may be a typical response; however, it can become a problem when it occurs too frequently or intensely, or leads to aggressive behaviour. When we understand it, however, anger can be controlled.

Because anger is a very acute emotion, many people are not aware that it involves a very subtle chain of events. The focus of anger-management training involves understanding and recognising these events, and intervening at different points in the chain

The process consists of:

A triggering event

↓

Our interpretation of the triggering event

↓

Physiological response

For example:

(Triggering event)

A boy walks across a clean floor with muddy feet

↓

(Interpretation of the triggering event)

The boy's mother thinks, 'Nobody appreciates the work I do to keep the house clean', and has a mental image of herself re-cleaning the floor, her back and legs aching.

↓

(Physiological response)

The mother's heart starts beating faster, her breathing becomes more rapid, and her muscles begin to feel tight.

→ Recognising triggers

When we understand what things are likely to trigger anger in us, it is easier for us to predict it. This can require careful consideration, because some events may only trigger anger when combined with some other factor or condition. For example, various circumstances can increase sensitivity to anger-triggering events (for example, tiredness, being in a crowded or noisy place, feeling hungry).

→ Cognitive Responses to Triggers

Become aware of the self-talk, or automatic thoughts, with which you respond to the events that typically trigger anger. When you are aware of the way you usually interpret or respond to such events you can challenge these interpretations for accuracy, and replace them with thoughts that can help maintain self-control.

The first step is to evaluate these thoughts to determine how realistic they are. Such thoughts are often absolutistic (for example, 'I'll always have to put up with this', or 'This never happens to other people'). Alternatively, these thoughts are often catastrophic (for example, 'This is just going to get worse and worse', 'I'm going to lose my mind if this keeps up').

The aim is to replace these automatic thoughts with more realistic ones. Question the thoughts by identifying evidence for and against the interpretation or expectation.

In addition to challenging the rationality of automatic thoughts, such thoughts can be replaced with coping statements. These are thoughts that can apply to a wide range of situations. They can be effective in reminding the individual that they are in control.

For example:

- ✔ I've gotten through this before, and I can do it again.
- ✔ Don't take it personally.
- ✔ This is going to be difficult, but I can handle it.
- ✔ Things are under control.

→ Recognising physiological responses

The physiological changes associated with anger can be addressed directly using relaxation techniques (for example, slow, deep breathing). However, as such responses escalate, this becomes increasingly difficult. It is therefore important to be able to recognise early physiological signs of anger so they can be addressed with minimal effort. The establishment of a regular relaxation routine can also decrease the likelihood of anger self-control difficulties.

→ Recognising Excessive Levels of Anger

Another important skill related to self-awareness is the ability to recognise when one's level of anger is so high that some kind of outburst is likely to soon occur. It is critical at such times to remove oneself from any environment in which people or belongings might be injured. ■

Module 3: Problem-Solving Skills

While the problems facing parents are many and varied, it is possible to apply the same set of steps to solving problems in general.

STEP 1: DEFINE THE PROBLEM

When you become aware of a problem, the first step is to form a clear idea of the ***outcome*** or ***goal*** that you are aiming for, and the issues that represent ***barriers*** to that outcome.

For example:

The problem for John's parents is that they have received a telephone call from his school principal, who has reported that John has been recently been getting into trouble for fighting with his peers.

The desired outcome for such a situation is for John to stop fighting.

There are a number of barriers to this outcome, things that make it hard for John's parents to reach this outcome. For example, they cannot personally supervise their son at the school, and they are not yet aware of the specific circumstances of the fighting.

STEP 2: BRAINSTORM SOLUTIONS

The next step is to think of what things might be done to overcome the identified barriers and reach the desired outcome. A number of potential solutions are generated using the ***brainstorm*** method. This means that ideas should be as creative and imaginative as possible, as they are not going to be evaluated at this point, but simply offered.

For example:

(1) Ask John about his behaviour in a warm and supportive manner

(2) Withdraw him from the school

(3) Telephone the school to find out more details about John's behaviour

(4) Send him to a psychiatrist

(5) Hire a private investigator to monitor John's behaviour

STEP 3: NARROW DOWN THE POTENTIAL SOLUTIONS

Each potential solution will vary in relation to feasibility, and each will result in different consequences. These must be considered when attempting to select the most appropriate course of action. Begin by eliminating those that appear obviously unrealistic, narrowing down the options to those most feasible.

For example:

(1) Possible

(2) Based on what is known there is no reason to go so far

(3) Possible

(4) First need to find out if he is the one causing the trouble, or if he is being bullied, and so on

(5) Too expensive

STEP 4: SELECT THE MOST APPROPRIATE SOLUTION

Consider the advantages and disadvantages of the remaining options.

For example:

Option 1 pros	Option 1 cons
The problem is addressed without without involving anyone outside the family	John might lie about his behaviour to avoid getting punished by his parents

STEP 5: CONSIDER HOW THE CHOSEN SOLUTION COULD BE IMPLEMENTED

Does it seem like a straightforward process, or are there other issues that must be first addressed? It may be the case that more than one of the generated solutions are chosen, and the order in which they are implemented may be relevant.

For example:

John's parents might decide to first implement option (1), and then follow this up with option (2).

Module 4: Pleasant Events and Social Support

For many parents, the care of their child represents the main focus of their activities. For stay-at-home parents, as well as those in paid employment, it is common for home- and child-related activities to limit their participation in activities of personal or social interest. Limited exposure to pleasant events or social interaction can adversely affect the wellbeing of parents and their ability to cope with the ongoing demands of parenting. In order to raise a well-balanced child, parents need to have a well-balanced life, with satisfying personal interests and social relationships.

THE BENEFITS OF ACTIVITY

- Feelings of fatigue resulting from child-focused activities can often be overcome by engaging in activities of personal enjoyment.
- Participating in personal activities can distract us from various issues that may be stressful.
- Participation in personal or social activities involves planning, and can therefore provide the opportunity to experience the satisfaction of achieving goals. This can improve motivation in relation to more general commitments.
- Taking yourself out of your everyday setting and into a new environment with different people can help to provide a new perspective on various issues or problems.
- Many enjoyable and relaxing activities involve interaction with other people. This can lead to the development of new friendships and greater social support.
- The experience of a depressed mood is often coupled with a lack of motivation and feelings of general disinterest. While this makes it harder to get involved in activities that are not routine, forcing oneself to engage in an activity that has previously been enjoyable is one of the most reliable ways to lift one's mood.

PLANNING ACTIVITIES

The process of participating in new activities involves a number of steps. There are also various guidelines that can be followed to get the most out of such activities.

When choosing activities, use a list such as that shown in the Pleasant Events Schedule. Consider both activities that have provided enjoyment in the past, perhaps before the children were born, as well as previously unattempted activities that appeal.

Include a mix of activities that can be enjoyed with minimal preparation and those requiring more planning. Rank these in order of how easy they will be to undertake.

While it is good to engage in these activities spontaneously when other commitments allow, for activities requiring preparation it is important to set aside time to participate in the activity. This may involve marking dates on calendars or in diaries. The most important step is to stick to these dates.

Attend to any other issues associated with the activity. This may involve arranging for child-minding, making bookings, obtaining particular materials, and so on.

One useful strategy for encouraging yourself to follow through with a planned event is to invite another person. People are less likely to cancel if it means having to explain why to someone else.

Enter the activity with an open mind. Maintain an attitude of experimentation, finding out what kind of things are enjoyable and satisfying. This can be useful for avoiding disappointment following an event. Remember that some activities will be more enjoyable than others, and that some people are more pleasant to be with than others. ■

Module 5: Cognitive Coping Skills

- All emotions are preceded by some thought or belief or interpretation.
- The 'situation' may be a very specific or subtle aspect of some set of circumstances, or an internal event such as a physiological sensation or a memory or thought.
- Thoughts are not always conscious; however, they can be accessed by asking yourself various questions.

A triggering event

↓

Our interpretation of the triggering event

↓

Physiological response

For example:

(Triggering event)

A boy walks across a clean floor with muddy feet

↓

(Interpretation of the triggering event)

The boy's mother thinks, 'Nobody appreciates the work I do to keep the house clean', and has a mental image of herself re-cleaning the floor, her back and legs aching.

↓

(Physiological response)

The mother's heart starts beating faster, her breathing becomes more rapid, and her muscles begin to feel tight.

AUTOMATIC THOUGHTS

- The term 'automatic thoughts' is used to describe all the spontaneous thoughts that run through our minds.
- These include both positive and negative thoughts that can be in the form of both verbal statements and images.
- These thoughts can be conscious and explicit, or unconscious and accessible only through self-questioning.
- Automatic thoughts may or may not make sense or be accurate or realistic.
- It is the negative automatic thoughts that are associated with a negative mood.
- Negative automatic thoughts often become more frequent in times of crisis or increased pressure.
- The negative automatic thoughts of people who suffer from depressed moods often contain errors (called logical errors) that create a negative bias.

IDENTIFYING AUTOMATIC THOUGHTS

1. When identifying automatic thoughts, express them as statements such as 'My child is going to end up is prison', rather than questions such as 'I wonder if my child will end up in prison'.
2. Attend to thoughts that correspond with a change or increase in emotion. These thoughts, or the changes in emotion they produce, may be distracting and interfere with the ability to concentrate on some task.
3. During an event, ask yourself questions such as:
   - What just went through my mind?
   - If I had to take a guess, what would I guess I was thinking about?
   - Am I picturing something in my mind?
4. When trying to access thoughts from a situation after it occurs, try to imagine yourself in that situation, describing the scenario in as much detail as possible, or imagining it as vividly as possible.
5. Define vague or ambiguous concepts (for example, What exactly do I mean by 'disaster'?).

CHALLENGING NEGATIVE AUTOMATIC THOUGHTS

The aim of challenging automatic thoughts is to replace the unrealistic assumptions or beliefs responsible for a negative mood with more realistic and hopeful alternatives.

Questioning automatic thoughts:

1. What is the evidence?

   What is the evidence that supports this idea?

   What is the evidence against this idea?
2. Is there an alternative explanation?
3. What is the worst that could happen? Could I live through it?

   What is the best that could happen?

   What is the most realistic outcome?
4. What is the effect of my believing the automatic thought?

   What could be the effect of changing my thinking?
5. What should I do about it?
6. What would I tell ________ (a friend) if they were in the same situation?

Identifying Automatic Thoughts When Looking Back on an Event

Thinking back to times when you noticed your mood change:

- Use a thoughts record form, recording the situation, automatic thoughts, emotions, adaptive responses, and emotional outcome.
- Plan to put yourself in situations that allow you to collect evidence in support of your new adaptive response.

At the time of a mood change:

- Take a moment to stop and identify automatic thoughts.
- Consider whether the current thoughts are similar to any that you have challenged previously, and make use of any previously successful responses.

OTHER USEFUL STRATEGIES

- Utilising coping statements. Take note of adaptive responses that can be applied to numerous negative thoughts. These can function as coping statements that may be useful while in the midst of a stressful situation in which there are limited opportunities to give attention to the specific automatic thoughts currently occurring.
- Maintaining a 'positives diary'. Keeping a positives diary involves recording positive events and experiences that disconfirm typical negative automatic thoughts. The aim of it is to compensate for the negative bias in automatic thoughts by shifting the balance in favour of thoughts that will enhance your self-esteem and increase motivation. For example, if you became aware of recurrent negative automatic thoughts related to your abilities as a parent (for example, 'I never do anything good for my child', or 'If my child misbehaves in public I won't know what to do'), your positives diary might include entries such as:

> Today I woke up early and took Aaron to the park. We both had a great time. Later we went shopping and he threw a tantrum when I wouldn't buy him a toy. I calmly explained my decision to him and followed through with it. He calmed down quite soon afterwards, and I realised that I am pretty prepared for situations like that. ■

Module 6: Partner Support Strategies

PART I: COMMON PROBLEMS AND WAYS TO OVERCOME THEM

ISSUE 1: Disagreement Over Household Rules

It is common for parents to have different expectations regarding the way children should behave. If you were to talk about the rules about behaviour that your own parents had when you were growing up, you would probably notice that there were different things that you were each allowed to get away with, and different things you were punished for.

However, different expectations about child behaviour can become a problem when parents enforce different rules with the same children. For example, if a father likes the children to take the initiative to do housework or cooking without being asked, while the mother wants the children to wait until they are asked so they can be supervised, it would be easy to understand the children getting into trouble for breaking the mother's rule. These kinds of mixed messages can be even more confusing to a child when parents argue about the rule in front of the child.

In this example the child probably would not respect the rule because his father does not. His mother's rule has been undermined by a parental disagreement. Children need to know the where, what, and how of behavioural rules. Children rely on their parents for these guidelines. It is therefore important to work together to agree on a set of household rules that you are both satisfied with.

ISSUE 2: Disagreement Over Discipline

Disagreement over the methods used to manage misbehaviour can also be confusing to children and result in increased misbehaviour. If punishment is inconsistent or varies in intensity it will not decrease the misbehaviour. On the contrary, it may often make the child behaviour even worse because the child feels that the punishment is unfair (for example, 'Last time nothing happened to me!'). If a child knows that punishment consistently follows misbehaviour, the behaviour is likely to decrease and the child will not feel hurt or discouraged by the punishment.

ISSUE 3: Fighting In Front of Children

While couples may fight from time to time, this is most likely to impact on children if it is happening in front of them. This is because children imitate their parents. If a child sees or hears yelling, requests being disregarded, or people being ignored, they will soon do the same. However, we can take advantage of this need to imitate by behaving with our partners the way we would like our children to behave with us and other people. If your children see you remaining calm, listening to others, and doing your best to help or comply with others, then they will do the same.

ISSUE 4: Not Sharing Workloads

There are many situations encountered regularly by parents that require more attention, hands, or eyes than one person is able to provide. During meal preparation, housework, and mealtimes, your attention is divided among different tasks and it is hard to supervise your children. It is no coincidence then that these are also the situations in which child behaviour is most likely to be a problem. However, difficulties with child behaviour can be decreased dramatically in such situations if the workload is divided between two parents with, for example, one parent minding the children while the other is occupied.

ISSUE 5: Being Tough Versus Being Soft

It is very important that both parents follow through with their own instructions to the child. It is good to back each other up as parents, but getting into the habit of relying on your partner to always discipline the children (or never discipline the children) is not good for either parent's relationship with the child.

We do not want the child to see one tough parent and one softy. We want the child to see two fair parents who expect to be listened to, and so on.

→ How to Act When a Child Misbehaves in the Presence of Both Parents

1. Remain calm.

   For example, use a calm voice when speaking to both the child and your partner.

2. Try not to interfere if your partner is dealing with the child.

   That is, don't 'come to the rescue' by being the tough partner. The parent who gave the instructions to the child should follow them through.

3. Help your partner if you can see they need it.

   For example, if your spouse is looking after one child and the other children start to misbehave, you could help by tending to the other children.

4. Back each other up by not giving contradictory instructions to the child.

   This is something that can require a bit of advance planning. So, take notice of situations in which you and your partner have different expectations of child behaviour, and come to a mutually satisfactory compromise.

5. Ensure that feedback you have for your partner is presented in a nonconfrontational way and provides constructive input.

   To do this, never comment on each other's behaviour until the problem is over and you are more relaxed. Also, try not to blame or criticise each other.

6. After the problem is over discuss it together and, if necessary, arrange a problem-solving discussion.

PART II: CASUAL DISCUSSIONS

Many of the problems that occur with couples are related to communication difficulties. Good communication practices can be important in any adult relationship, but when the couple are relying on each other to do something as involved as raising a child, effective communication becomes absolutely critical.

One way of maintaining good communication is by putting aside a little time each day to talk to each other about the children and any other family matters. We use the term 'casual discussions' to refer to discussions that are not deliberately organised, but occur regularly at times when one or both partners would like to share information.

We are going to look at a specific way of structuring discussions that maximises mutual understanding about your attitudes and behaviours as parents, and helps you to encourage and support each other in your child-management efforts.

While most parents attempt to discuss general family matters on a regular basis, these discussions can often be ineffective due to a number of things.

ISSUE 1: No Actual Discussion Takes Place

This can occur in a number of common scenarios. For example, a home-duties parent may try to report the events of the day to a working partner as soon as they step through the door. Alternatively, a working parent may try to engage a home-duties partner in a discussion requiring concerted thought when the partner has their first opportunity to relax after running around after the children.

Whatever the reason may be, when parents stop talking regularly family rifts begin, and it is likely that:

- parents will not present a united front to their children
- parents will not be consistent in their child-management techniques
- family problems will grow rather than disappear
- children will consistently misbehave.

ISSUE 2: Discussions Do Not Change Anything

A second common problem occurs when parents frequently discuss child-related issues and difficulties yet nothing eventuates from these discussions and things do not improve.

There are three common explanations for this:

1. During the discussion problems are identified, but no solution is reached, and no plans are made.
2. Parents disagree about what the problem is, or even disagree that there is a problem.
3. One parent may feel that the problem only occurs with the other parent. As such, they do not listen to the discussion; they are not interested.

ISSUE 3: Discussions Are Unpleasant

Like any other activity, if discussions are unpleasant people will do their best to avoid them. Unfortunately, such avoidance can occur at the times at which discussions may be most useful, such as following family outings. The main reasons that discussions are aversive include nagging, ignoring, ridicule, and sarcasm.

However, if these discussions are conducted in a certain way they can become an important way of supporting and encouraging each other.

First, it is important to make sure that you speak to each other every day, at a time that is convenient for both partners; for example, when you get home from work, after an outing, or during dinner. However, the important thing is to make an agreement about such times rather than assuming that the chosen time is convenient for the other partner.

Second, try to follow the steps for conducting casual discussions listed over the page. You will note that this routine encourages you to listen to each other, to provide feedback on each other's behaviour, to ask questions of each other, and to schedule a problem-solving session if necessary. Do not try to solve any problems during these discussions. Just take time to listen to each other. If something good happened, praise it and enjoy your partner's success. If something unpleasant happened, get the details and offer to help, as suggested over the page.

→ Steps for Conducting Casual Discussions

- ✔ Ask your partner about their day
- ✔ Show you are listening and interested
- ✔ Ask how the children have been in your absence

IF NO PROBLEM OCCURRED

↓

Ask what the children have been doing and give positive feedback to your partner.

IF A PROBLEM OCCURRED

↓

Ask for a clear description of what happened. Listen carefully and show that you are listening and interested.

- ✔ Ask how your partner dealt with the situation.
- ✔ Again, show you are listening and interested.

IF THE PROBLEM WAS HANDLED IN A WAY CONSISTENT WITH THE PROGRAM

↓

Give positive feedback to your partner.

IF YOUR PARTNER HAD TROUBLE HANDLING THE PROBLEM

↓

1. Give positive feedback on any successful aspects of how they handled the problem.
2. Make a time to sit down together and have a problem-solving discussion.

- ✔ Finally, offer to do something to help avoid the problem next time (for example, looking after your son while your wife bathes your daughter).

PART III: PROBLEM-SOLVING DISCUSSIONS

As parents, you cannot avoid all problems, but you can prevent them from developing into severe problems, and you can overcome many as well. Following are a number of common difficulties encountered when attempting problem-solving discussions, and guidelines for conducting problem-solving discussions:

ISSUE 1: Disagreement Over the Problem

What is a problem to one person may not be a problem to another. In order to solve a problem, the most fundamental requirement is that both partners agree on what it is.

There are no easy solutions to this issue, but the first step is to sit down and talk about it. This means saying how you feel about the situation and listening to the other's point of view. The goals should be to reach a mutually agreeable definition of what is acceptable to both partners, and what is not. At times, a compromise may be the only solution.

ISSUE 2: Disagreement Over the Solution

After agreeing on what needs to change, the next step is to identify potential solutions. Disagreement can be a common difficulty at this step. One parent might believe that waiting is the most appropriate way to handle the problem, while the other might feel that it needs to be addressed immediately.

A useful approach at this stage is to write down all possible solutions, and then discuss them one at a time before making any decisions. Weigh up the pros and cons of each potential solution, having your say and listening to your partner's view. The process of agreeing on the most appropriate solution may involve compromise and, when possible, the most effective way of identifying the best solution is to put it into practice and observe the outcome.

ISSUE 3: Disagreement Over the Implementation of the Solution

The next step is to translate the agreed-upon course of action into a practical plan so that each of you knows exactly what to do when the problem occurs.

Implementing a course of action in a consistent way is particularly important, as a failure to do so can prevent you from finding out how useful the agreed- upon solution actually is.

Provide each other with plenty of encouragement and motivation, and keep an open mind. If the intended course of action falls short of the goal, do not get discouraged. Arrange another problem-solving discussion and try again. Sooner or later you will find the solution that works.

ISSUE 4: Difficulties Finding the Time and the Place

To be conducted effectively, problem-solving discussions require a high degree of concentration and cooperation. You cannot achieve this unless you are comfortable and relaxed and can work uninterrupted. As such, it is essential that you and your partner can negotiate a mutually convenient time when you can be alone and will not be interrupted by children or other commitments.

This might mean waiting until the children are in bed and you can spread out any paperwork over a table.

ISSUE 4: Difficulties Finding the Time and the Place (CONTINUED)

GUIDELINES FOR CONDUCTING PROBLEM-SOLVING DISCUSSIONS

- ✔ **Agree** upon a mutual time and place to talk to each other about any problems you are currently experiencing. It should be when you are both calm and will not be interrupted by the children.
- ✔ **Identify** the problem behaviour as specifically as possible. Try to deal with one problem at a time. Write down the problem as clearly as possible. Check that you both agree on what needs to change.
- ✔ **Brainstorm** together, thinking of as many possible solutions as you can, and write these down clearly.
- ✔ **Discuss** each solution, weighing its pros and cons, its likelihood of success, whether it is practical to use, and any problems that might arise.
- ✔ **Choose** the best solution(s) by mutual agreement or compromise.
- ✔ **Plan** a strategy for using the solution. Be specific in working out exactly what you will both say and do when the problem occurs.
- ✔ Plan to **review** how the solution is going by arranging another meeting together.

PART IV: GIVING AND RECEIVING FEEDBACK

GUIDELINES FOR GIVING CONSTRUCTIVE FEEDBACK

Giving effective feedback to each other involves communicating opinions in a way that makes your partner feel good about your ideas, and helps them change their behaviour for the better. These aims can only be achieved by knowing how to speak and listen effectively. However, these skills can be learnt by following a number of basic guidelines:

1. **Start with the positives**. When offering feedback, it helps the receiver to first hear what you liked about their behaviour. If the positive is heard first, the negative is more likely to be listened to, and acted upon. For example:

   'I felt you did the right thing by putting John into time-out when he was screaming. I did feel you were a bit rough with him when you pushed him into the room, however.'

2. **Be specific.** Try to avoid general or vague comments. Statement such as 'You were brilliant' or 'Try harder next time' do not give any details and are therefore of limited use in helping the person change. Try to pinpoint exactly what the person did rather than using general labels or suggestions. For example:

   'You spoke in a very pleasant voice when he was misbehaving today.'

   or

   'I feel that you kept arguing with John when you could have acted and used back-up such as time-out.'

3. **Offer alternatives.** Suggest at least one thing that the person could have done differently. In doing so, turn the negative into a positive suggestion. For example:

   'I felt that instead of ignoring Judy's swearing, you could have told her you didn't like it, and backed up your instruction.'

PART IV: GIVING AND RECEIVING FEEDBACK (CONTINUED)

GUIDELINES FOR GIVING CONSTRUCTIVE FEEDBACK (CONTINUED)

4. **Describe, do not judge.** Describe what happened, not your judgment of whether it was 'good', 'bad', 'nasty', 'nice', and so forth. For example:

   'You are using child-directed play techniques really well when you play with the children and it really seems to be helping them to play cooperatively.'

   is better than

   'You play well with the children.'

5. **Own the feedback.** It is easy to say to the other person 'you are ...', as if you are offering a universally agreed-upon opinion. Remember that when you are giving feedback it is your opinion, and thus it is better to start with openings like:

   'I feel that ...'

   'In my opinion ...'

GUIDELINES FOR RECEIVING FEEDBACK

While we may think of ourselves as being in a passive role when it is our turn to receive feedback, it is important that we know how to make the most out of the feedback provided, and to remember that the purpose of feedback is to improve the way we do things.

So, we are going to look now at things you can do to get the most out of feedback from your partner. These guidelines can also be used in other settings:

1. **Listen to the feedback rather than immediately rejecting or arguing with it.** While it can be uncomfortable to hear, it can result in positive outcomes. Remember that people do have their opinions about you. They will have their own perceptions of your behaviour, and it can help to be aware of these.
2. **Be clear about what is being said.** Try to avoid jumping to conclusions or becoming immediately defensive, otherwise people may limit their feedback or you may not be able to make full use of it. Make sure you understand the feedback before you respond to it. A useful technique can be to paraphrase or repeat the feedback, to check that you have understood.
3. **Ask for the feedback you want but do not get.** If feedback pertaining to important activities is not provided, it is important to elicit it. The feedback initially provided may be restricted to one aspect of our behaviour and we may have to request specific feedback that is not volunteered.
4. **Decide what you will do as a result of the feedback.** Remember that the aim of receiving feedback is to help us change our behaviour for the better. So when feedback is available, consider how you might behave next time the situation occurs. In this way, the feedback will not be wasted.

SECTION 4:
References

References

Ainsworth, M.D.S., Blehar, M.C., Waters, E., & Wall, S. (1978). *Patterns of attachment: A psychological study of the strange situation.* Hillsdale, NJ: Erlbaum.

American Psychiatric Association. (1994). *Diagnostic and statistical manual of mental disorders* (4th ed.). Washington, DC: Author.

Bakermans-Kranenburg, M.J., & van IJzendoorn, M.H. (1993). A psychometric study of the adult attachment interview: Reliability and discriminant validity. *Developmental Psychology, 29*(5), 870–879.

Barrett, P.M., Dadds, M.R., & Rapee, R.M. (1996). Family treatment of childhood anxiety: A controlled trial. *Journal of Consulting and Clinical Psychology, 64*(2), 333–342.

Beauchaine, T.P., Webster-Stratton, C., & Reid, M. (2005). Mediators, moderators, and predictors of one-year outcomes among children treated for early-onset conduct problems: A latent growth curve analysis. *Journal of Consulting and Clinical Psychology, 73*(3), 371–388.

Brestan, E.V., & Eyberg, S.M. (1998). Effective psychosocial treatments of conduct-disordered children and adolescents: 29 years, 82 studies, and 5272 children. *Journal of Clinical Child Psychology, 27*(2), 180–189.

Bowlby, J. (1969), *Attachment, Vol. 1 of Attachment and loss.* London: Hogarth Press.

Cowan, P.A., Cohn, D.A., Cowan, C.P., & Pearson, J.L. (1996). Parents' attachment histories and children's externalizing and internalizing behaviors: Exploring family systems models of linkage. *Journal of Consulting and Clinical Psychology, 64*(1), 53–63.

Dadds, M.R. (1995). *Families, children, and the development of dysfunction.* Newbury Park, CA: Sage Press.

Dadds, M.R. (2002). Learning and intimacy in the families of anxious children. In R.J. McMahon & R.D. Peters (Eds.), *The effects of parental dysfunction on children* (pp. 87–106). New York, NY: Kluwer Academic.

Dadds, M.R., Mullins, M.J., McAllister, R.A., & Atkinson, E. (2003). Attributions, affect, and behavior in abuse-risk mothers: A laboratory study. *Child Abuse and Neglect, 27*(1), 21–45.

Dadds, M.R., Sanders, M.R., Behrens, B.C., & James J.E. (1987). Marital discord and child behaviour problems: A description of family interactions during treatment. *Journal of Clinical Child Psychology, 16*(3), 192–203.

Dadds, M.R., Schwartz, S., & Sanders, M.R. (1987). Marital discord and treatment outcome in the treatment of childhood conduct disorders. *Journal of Consulting and Clinical Psychology, 55*(3), 396–403.

DeKlyen, M., Speltz, M.L., & Greenberg, M.T. (1998). Fathering and early onset conduct problems: Positive and negative parenting, father-son attachment, and the marital context. *Clinical Child and Family Psychology Review, 1*(1), 3–21.

Dishion, T.J., & Patterson, G.R. (1992). Age effects in parent training outcome. *Behavior Therapy, 23,* 719–729.

Erickson, M.F., Sroufe, L.A., & Egeland, B. (1985). The relationship between the quality of attachment and behaviour problems in preschool in a high-risk sample. In I. Bretherton & E. Waters (Eds.), Growing points of attachment theory and research. *Monographs of the Society for Research in Child Development, 50*(1–2, Serial No. 209), 147–167.

Farmer, E.Z.M., Compton, S.N., Burns, B.J., & Robertson, E. (2002). Review of the evidence base for treatment of childhood psychopathology: Externalizing disorders. *Journal of Counseling and Community Psychology, 70*(6), 1267–1302.

Frick, P.J., & Morris, A.S. (2004). Temperament and developmental pathways to severe conduct problems. *Journal of Clinical Child and Adolescent Psychology, 33*(1), 54–68.

Green, S.M., Loeber, R., & Lahey, B.B. (1992). Child psychopathology and deviant family hierarchies. *Journal of Child and Family Studies, 1*(3), 341–350.

Greenberg, M.T., Speltz, L., & DeKlyen, M. (1993). The role of attachment in the early development of disruptive behavior problems. *Development and Psychopathology, 5*, 191–213.

Harlow, H.F., & Harlow, M. (1962). Social deprivation in monkeys. *Scientific American, 207*, 136–146.

Henggeler, S.W., Melton, G.B., & Smith, L.A. (1992). Family preservation using multisystemic therapy: An effective alternative to incarcerating serious juvenile offenders. *Journal of Consulting and Clinical Psychology, 60*(6), 953–961.

Lamb, M. (Ed.). (1997). Fathers and child development: An introductory overview and guide. In *The role of the father in child development* (pp. 1–18). New York: John Wiley & Sons.

Lyons-Ruth, K. (1996). Attachment relationships among children with aggressive behaviour problems: The role of disorganized early attachment patterns. *Journal of Consulting and Clinical Psychology, 64*(1), 64–73.

Lyons-Ruth, K., Alpern, L., & Repacholi, B. (1993). Disorganised infant attachment classification and maternal psychosocial problems as predictors of hostile-aggressive behaviour in the preschool classroom. *Child Development, 64*(2), 572–585.

Lyons-Ruth, K., Repacholi, B., McLeod, S., & Silva, E. (1991). Disorganized attachment behavior in infancy: Short-term stability, maternal and infant correlates and risk-related sub-types. *Development and Psychopathology, 3*, 207–266.

McMahon, R.J., & Forehand, R. (2003). *Helping the non-compliant child: Family-based treatment for oppositional behaviour* (2nd ed.). New York: Guilford Press.

McNeil, C.B., Eyberg, S.M., Eisenstadt, T.H., Newcomb, K., & Funderburk, B.W. (1991). Parent-child interaction therapy with behaviour problem children: Generalisation of treatment effects to the school setting. *Journal of Clinical Child Psychology, 20*(2), 140–151.

Miller, G.E., & Prinz, R.J. (1990). Enhancement of social learning family interventions for child conduct disorder. *Psychological Bulletin, 108*(2), 291–307.

Minuchin, S. (1974). *Families and family therapy*. Cambridge: Harvard University Press.

Nixon, R.D.V., Sweeney, L., Erickson, D.B., & Touyz, S.W. (2004). Parent-child interaction therapy: A comparison of standard and abbreviated treatments for oppositional defiant preschoolers. *Journal of Consulting and Clinical Psychology, 71*(2), 251–260.

Patterson, G.R. (1982). A *social learning approach: 3. Coercive family process*. Eugene, OR: Castalia.

Patterson, G.R., & Chamberlain, P. (1994). A functional analysis of resistance during parent training therapy. *Clinical Psychology and Scientific Practice, 1*, 53–70.

Patterson, G.R., & Gullion, M.E. (1968). *Living with children: New methods for parents and teachers*. Champaign, IL: Research Press.

Patterson, G.R., & Reid, J.B. (1984). Social interaction processes within the family: The study of the moment-by-moment family transactions in which human development is embedded. *Journal of Applied Developmental Psychology, 5*(3), 237–262.

Reid, J.B., Patterson, G.R., & Snyder, J.J. (2002). *Antisocial behaviour in children and adolescents: A developmental analysis and model for intervention*. Washington, DC: American Psychological Association.

Robin, A.L. (1981). A controlled evaluation of problem solving communication training with parent–adolescent conflict. *Behavior Therapy, 12*, 593–609.

Ruma, P.R., Burke, R.V., & Thompson, R.W. (1996). Group parent training: Is it effective for children of all ages? *Behavior Therapy, 27*, 159–169.

Sanders, M.R., & Dadds, M.R. (1993). *Behavioural family intervention*. Needham Heights, MA: Allyn & Bacon.

Sanders, M.R., Dadds, M.R., & Bor, W. (1989). Contextual analysis of child oppositional and maternal aversive behaviours in families of conduct disordered and non-problem children. *Journal of Clinical Child Psychology, 18*(1), 72–83.

Sanders, M.R., & Glynn, T. (1981). Training parents in behavioural self-management: An analysis of generalisation and maintenance. *Journal of Applied Behaviour Analysis, 14*, 223–237.

Sanders, M.R., Markie-Dadds, C., Tully, L.A., & Bor, W. (2000). The Triple-P-Positive Parenting Program: A comparison of enhanced, standard, and self-directed behavioural family intervention for parents of children with early onset conduct problems. *Journal of Consulting and Clinical Psychology, 68*(4), 624–640.

Sanders, M.R., Markie-Dadds, C., & Turner, K.M.T. (2003). Theoretical, scientific and clinical foundations of the Triple P-Positive-Parenting Program: A population approach to the promotion of parenting competence. *Parenting Research and Practice Monograph, 1*(1), 1–21.

Serketich, W.J., & Dumas, J.E. (1996). The effectiveness of behavioural parent training to modify antisocial behaviour in children. A meta-analysis. *Behavior Therapy, 27*(2), 171–186.

Shaw, D.S., Bell, R.Q., & Gilliom, M. (2000). A truly early starter model of antisocial behaviour revisited. *Clinical Child and Family Psychology Review, 3*(3), 155–172.

Snyder, J., & Stoolmiller, M. (2002). Reinforcement and coercive mechanisms in the development of antisocial behaviour. The family. In J. Reid, G. Patterson, & J. Snyder (Eds.), *Antisocial behaviour in children and adolescents: A developmental analysis and model for intervention* (pp. 65–100). Washington, DC: American Psychological Association.

Task Force on Promotion and Dissemination of Psychological Procedures. (1995). Training in and dissemination of empirically-validated treatments: Report and recommendations. *The Clinical Psychologist, 48*(1), 3–23.

Wahler, R.G., & Dumas, J.E. (1989). Attentional problems in dysfunctional mother-child interactions: An interbehavioral model. *Psychological Bulletin, 105*(1), 116–130.

Waugh, L., & Sanders, M.R. (Producers/Directors). (1993). *Family Observation Schedule: Observer training tape.* [Videotape]. Brisbane: Behaviour Research and Therapy Centre, The University of Queensland.

Webster-Stratton, C. (1994). Advancing videotape parent training: A comparison study. *Journal of Consulting and Clinical Psychology, 62*(3), 583–593.

Webster-Stratton, C. (1996). Early-onset conduct problems: Does gender make a difference? *Journal of Consulting and Clinical Psychology, 64*(3), 540–551.

Webster-Stratton, C., & Hammond, M. (1997). Treating children with early-onset conduct problems: A comparison of child and parent training interventions. *Journal of Consulting and Clinical Psychology, 65*(1), 93–109.

Webster-Stratton, C., Kolpacoff, M., & Hollinsworth, T. (1989). The long-term effectiveness and clinical significance of three cost-effective training programs for families with conduct problem children. *Journal of Consulting and Clinical Psychology, 57*(4), 550–553.

Williams, K.D., & Zadro, L. (2001). Ostracism: On being ignored, excluded and rejected. In M. Leary (Ed.), *Interpersonal rejection* (pp. 21–53). New York: Oxford University Press.

Youngblade, L.M., & Belsky, J. (1992). Parent-child antecedents of five-year-olds' close friendships: A longitudinal analysis. *Developmental Psychology, 28*(4), 700–713.

Notes

CPSIA information can be obtained at www.ICGtesting.com
Printed in the USA
BVOW06s0330250214

345937BV00005B/153/P

9 781875 378586